WHEN IN DOUBT, MAKE BELIEF

AN OCD–INSPIRED APPROACH TO LIVING WITH UNCERTAINTY

**Field-Tested
(and Re-Tested and Re-Re-Tested)
Strategies for Confronting Fear and Worry**

JEFF BELL

author of *Rewind, Replay, Repeat*

Foreword by Michael A. Jenike, MD

PRAISE FOR *WHEN IN DOUBT, MAKE BELIEF*

"If you know people who double back in their car to check if their garage door is closed, tell them about this book. It's a much-needed work."
— Larry King, author of *The Best of Larry King Live*
and *My Remarkable Journey*

"This book is not just for those with OCD but for all of us who have suffered in this life and who wish to make some sense of it all. Well written and quite uplifting."
— Sharon Salzberg, author of
Lovingkindness: The Revolutionary Art of Happiness

"Jeff Bell's writing is compassionate, direct, and articulate. His system of personal transformation is crafted out of the grit of personal OCD experience. The result is an inspiring and powerful program that shows us all how to lead a more meaningful and passionate life. This is a great book!"
— Maria Nemeth, PhD, MCC, author of
The Energy of Money and *Mastering Life's Energies*

"More than insightful, Jeff Bell's *When in Doubt, Make Belief* is at once humble, human, practical, thoughtful, and masterful. Through vignettes, examples, and a rigorous but intuitive set of guidelines for encountering and countering doubt — whether in the context of OCD or other life dilemmas — Bell shows how focusing on the big picture, and the Greater Good, can lead us out of blind alleys and self-imposed traps. My strongest recommendation."
— Stephen Hinshaw, PhD, psychology department chair,
University of California, Berkeley

"An extremely well-written book that provides an exquisite understanding of OCD while teaching valuable concepts and tools to overcome fear. Through his own inspirational personal story and extensive research, Bell offers the reader a way to tap into a sense of certainty and clarity to push through uncertainty and doubts."
— Christine Hassler, life coach and author of
20 Something, 20 Everything

PRAISE FOR JEFF BELL'S *REWIND, REPLAY, REPEAT*

"Jeff Bell is an excellent and experienced radio newsman. But of all the many fascinating stories he has reported over the years, none is more bizarre or more compelling than the one he tells here. Furthermore, it is an exclusive. Only Bell could possibly tell it because it is an account of his own struggle with his own worst enemy, whose name is Doubt."

— Charles Osgood, CBS News *Sunday Morning* anchor

"The best first-person account available on life from the point of view of the OCD sufferer."

— Jeffrey M. Schwartz, MD, author of *Brain Lock*

"A page-turner for anyone interested in obsessive compulsive disorder. Beautifully written and gripping in its intensity, it takes the reader on the perilous adventure of the fight against OCD. Jeff Bell enlists us on his journey: his sense of humor, irony, and reporting skills make this book a must-read."

— Judith L. Rapoport, MD, author of
The Boy Who Couldn't Stop Washing

"Bell's story provides plenty of lessons, perspective, and hope for those living with OCD — either their own or someone else's — in a funny, highly entertaining narrative."

— *Publishers Weekly*

WHEN IN DOUBT, MAKE BELIEF

WHEN IN DOUBT, MAKE BELIEF

AN OCD-INSPIRED APPROACH TO LIVING WITH UNCERTAINTY

Jeff Bell

Foreword by Michael A. Jenike, MD

New World Library
Novato, California

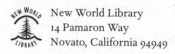 New World Library
14 Pamaron Way
Novato, California 94949

Text design by Tona Pearce Myers
Author photo on back cover by John Barkey, www.ClimbAMountain.com.

Library of Congress Cataloging-in-Publication Data
Bell, Jeff.
  When in doubt, make belief : an OCD-inspired approach to living with uncertainty / Jeff Bell ; foreword by Michael A. Jenike.
    p.   cm.
Includes bibliographical references and index.
ISBN 978-1-57731-670-1 (pbk. : alk. paper)
1. Obsessive-compulsive disorder. 2. Belief and doubt. 3. Uncertainty. 4. Anxiety. I. Title.
  RC533.B455 2009
  616.85'227—dc22   2009027092

First printing, October 2009
ISBN 978-1-57731-670-1
Printed in Canada on 100% postconsumer-waste recycled paper

New World Library is a proud member of the Green Press Initiative.

10   9   8   7   6   5   4   3   2   1

For all who dare to believe . . .
beyond the doubt

Contents

PART THREE: CHOOSING GREATER GOOD

Foreword

I first ran across Jeff Bell when he gave the keynote talk at the Obsessive Compulsive Foundation annual meeting in Houston in 2007 and discussed his popular book *Rewind, Replay, Repeat: A Memoir of Obsessive-Compulsive Disorder*. Jeff received a tremendous ovation, and the audience, largely consisting of patients with OCD, was delighted at his personal progress and by his recommendations for them. He talked about ways to manage OCD as well as the need for OCD sufferers to give back and help others in order to help themselves. He talked openly about his own OCD and how it had sucked the life out of him.

Working with OCD patients since the late 1970s, I have seen some remain very ill, thousands of patients get moderately better, and a few make dramatic strides and totally reclaim their lives. It has seemed to me that the ones who do best are those who feel obligated to give back and help other patients. Somehow this drive to help others energizes them to fight off their own OCD and stay well and productive. The fact that Jeff was saying this same thing resonated with me.

After his talk, the OC Foundation board of directors asked Jeff to meet with them; and when they came to appreciate his skills and his drive to help others, they asked him to join the board and become a national spokesperson for the foundation.

I was delighted to hear of this new book, which explores the life lessons that OCD and its treatment have to offer and the motivational framework that Jeff has developed. Jeff is a clear thinker and an excellent communicator. His book is an easy read and very well written, and the concepts it presents can help all of us, whether or not we have OCD.

As he explains, Jeff reached a point in his life where he could stand OCD no more: "Show me how to turn around this crazy life," he mumbled to the universe, "and I'll share my story with anyone who will listen." In the weeks that followed, he reports, something profound did indeed happen: "I somehow turned that bargain on its head." And that's when he "first stumbled onto the concept of Greater Good and the very key to making belief." He decided that his life would be driven by two distinct objectives: first, to enhance his own sense of purpose (by giving meaning to all he had been through in his OCD battles), and second, to be of service to others (by offering a first-person account of living with, and recovering from, the very worst of this disorder). These concepts of *purpose* and *service* would prove to be the most powerful motivators behind his OCD recovery and outreach.

The question of how to motivate people with OCD has plagued clinicians for decades. We can offer treatments that work, but we cannot get some of the patients who need them the most to engage in the treatment process wholeheartedly. This book goes a long way toward motivating patients and makes a significant contribution to the treatment of OCD. It also has something to offer all of us in these uncertain times, since what helps motivate someone to confront OCD doubt can also help people without OCD confront life's uncertainty.

As Jeff notes, "If you picked up this book looking for easy solutions to dealing with uncertainty — well, I'm afraid you're out of luck." The approach he is advocating works; he knows that from first-hand experience. But, as he warns, it's far from easy.

I think you will enjoy *When in Doubt, Make Belief* and find it immensely helpful.

Michael A. Jenike, MD
Chair, OC Foundation Scientific Advisory Board
Professor of Psychiatry, Harvard Medical School

Introduction

"Raise your hand if you've ever driven away from your house and found yourself wondering whether you really closed the garage door."

I've made this request of audiences across the country, and I'm always fascinated by the response. Almost without exception, hands go up. Heads nod. Shared laughs fill the room.

"Now raise your hand," I ask, "if you've ever doubled back to check the garage door." Typically, there's a collective pause at this point, followed by a succession of arms inching upward. Soon I am again looking at a sea of hands, again hearing a chorus of laughs.

"Okay," I say, "one last request: Raise your hand if you've doubled back to your garage, checked it, driven off, and then needed to drive back to check it yet again."

Nothing.

Hands stay in laps. Eyebrows rise. Glances are exchanged.

"Ahhhhh," I say, drawing out the word for dramatic effect. "*This* is what separates me from most of you."

As I go on to explain, *I* have indeed driven back to my garage a second and even a third time on far too many occasions, only to drive off each time even more uncertain, seemingly unable to store whatever sensory input might convince me that the door is actually closed.

Why?

That's a question, really, for the neuroscientists who study brain structure, neurotransmission, and the like. The short answer, however, is simple: I am one of the millions of Americans battling obsessive compulsive disorder, or OCD, a biochemical brain disorder marked by intrusive recurring thoughts and nonsensical rituals aimed at dislodging these thoughts. This condition is often called the "doubting disease," and for good reason. Brains like mine are predisposed to question sensory data, to check on it time and again, and to struggle mightily in the absence of proven treatments.

In early 2007 I went public with my story in all its gory detail. After years of living an elaborate and exhausting double life as a successful radio news anchor secretly consumed by endless obsessions and compulsions, I put it all out there in a memoir titled *Rewind, Replay, Repeat*. On its pages I shared my earliest memories of OCD, my spiral into the worst of chronic doubt in my late twenties, my misdiagnoses and other misadventures in seeking treatment, my discovery of a book that gave my challenges a name, and my long and circuitous road to wellness.

Never could I have imagined just how widespread the interest in my story would be. Week after week, on the radio and television, in newspapers and magazines, at bookstores and libraries, and at national conventions and neighborhood service clubs, I shared my story with audiences, always marveling at their interest and their questions. Something about the topic intrigued them. Initially I assumed it was the freak-show factor — the bizarre nature of my distorted thinking and the even more bizarre nature of my rituals. Let's face it, there's something weirdly fascinating about a guy who drives his car in circles or can't pry himself away from a sink. This, I was certain, was what kept audiences showing up for my talks and spending their hard-earned money on my book.

I was wrong. The reality, I've come to understand, is that it's the familiarity of my story, not the strangeness, that strikes a chord in so many people. Call it the "There but by the grace of God go I" factor. Tales of schizophrenia, multiple personality disorder, and other mental health problems may titillate "normal" (i.e., mentally healthy) readers, but seldom do such stories leave them contemplating the links between their own cognitive and behavioral patterns and the pathological extremes. I couldn't even begin to estimate how many times I've been asked if a reader's own quirks — arranging socks, counting steps, checking toasters — could constitute clinical OCD.

This connection I realized on my own, if only slowly. Over a much longer period, and with the input of many friends and readers, I reached two other conclusions: first, that the lessons I've learned from living with chronic uncertainty apply not only to battling obsessions and compulsions but also to dealing with everyday doubts and our often counterproductive reactions to them; and second, that the principles of applied belief that served as guiding beacons through my own darkest years can also offer a way out of the shadows of all kinds of doubt.

The more I thought about all these connections, the more I began to see what a powerful laboratory OCD offers for understanding the mechanics of belief. And if those of us toiling away in this lab by default — that is, because of our biological predisposition to doubt — are somehow able to train ourselves to accept uncertainty and believe beyond the flawed processing of our cross-wired brains, shouldn't *anyone* be able to?

The answer, I'm now convinced, is a resounding but qualified Yes — qualified only because that *anyone* must also be willing to do what we with OCD, out of necessity, have had to do — namely, learn how to *make belief.*

For me, this learning process took many, many years and an enormous toll on my life. It cost me thousands of dollars, and it nearly cost me everything most dear to me. But it didn't have to; I just happened to be a little slow to catch on to some fundamental principles that were right in front of me all along — principles that came to serve as building blocks in the construction of my own model of applied belief and, ultimately, rescued me from the depths of the doubt-filled morass that was my life.

It is these principles — so basic, but powerful — that I hope to impart in the chapters that follow. And to that end, I want to share with you just how they came together for me, and how I learned to apply them during what I now call my Crash Course in Believing.

But while my own story provides the backbone for this book, there are many other stories I also want to share. These are stories I've been privileged to collect while traveling the country talking about OCD and chronic doubt. They illustrate how people from all walks of life — doctors, athletes, stay-at-home moms, business managers, and celebrities — have drawn on these same principles to live with, and even thrive amidst, the uncertainty in their worlds.

Black and white **is a term** you'll see frequently in the coming pages. It describes an OCD sufferer's world better than any other I can offer. Something about our brain wiring just seems to lead us to see life and all of its components as an endless string of dichotomies. Things appear to us to be either good or bad, right or wrong, black or white. For much of my life, this was a curse, and it certainly clouded my thinking on many fronts. In retrospect, though, I can also appreciate how it allowed me to explore so deeply what I've come to define as the polar opposite of doubt: namely, belief. Because this particular dichotomy is so central to the lessons of my story, I have structured this book accordingly. In part 1, I offer all that I know about doubt and its impacts. In part 2, I delineate ten specific strategies I've developed for making belief. And in part 3, I share the Greater Good motivational technique I've used to shift my decision making from doubt-driven to belief-driven, and I introduce you to five remarkable individuals who demonstrate this ability in the face of great uncertainty.

I think you'll find that reading this book is much like taking a journey. To keep us on track, I have enlisted the help of more than a dozen experts — specialists in a variety of fields, from psychology and brain science to religion and history. I hope their insights will serve as guideposts, and I encourage you to read their sidebars along the way.

I'd like to promise you that once you've completed this journey, you'll never check your garage door again, but I'm afraid I can't. For all I know, you did indeed leave it open this morning. (Sorry!) What I can predict with great confidence is this: if you apply the principles of belief in these pages, doubt *will* loosen its grip on your life. And if you find yourself questioning that, you are indeed holding the right book in your hands!

PART ONE

IN (THE SHADOW OF) DOUBT

CHAPTER ONE

With or Within Doubt?

Intellect-Based vs. Fear-Based Doubt

Dark and cold is the Shadow of Doubt,
with the winds of fear whipping about...

I can't recall just when I wrote these words — the start of some unfinished poem that looped in my head for many years — but I do know exactly where I was: deep in the recesses of a frigid blackness I would come to associate with uncertainty — the chronic, crushing variety that those of us with OCD know all too well.

This place, this Shadow of Doubt, is hardly the exclusive territory of OCD sufferers. I know from the many stories I've collected over the years that doubt casts a shadow across all kinds of life challenges, from issues of physical and mental health to those posed by the simple rigors of everyday living. I think it's safe to say that almost everyone has experienced, at some point or another, at least a glimpse of the darkness and a tinge of the chill that uncertainty can prompt.

That said, I also think that those of us who have battled severe OCD have an intimate knowledge of this shadow that few others can appreciate. We who have spent years lost in the darkness of doubt know what it's like to be utterly consumed by uncertainty, stripped of even the most basic human sensibilities that would offer us a way back to the light. This is why I want to introduce you to the OCD world and the view from its darkest corners. With the help of a handful of others who share my challenges, and a number of the world's top experts who make their livings studying and helping people like me, I hope to offer you a guided tour of the Shadow of Doubt, with an insider's perspective and an eye toward the trapdoors and funhouse-like distortions awaiting us at every turn.

But first, let me offer a few words about a key distinction we need to make when talking about doubt and the roles that it plays in our lives.

HEALTHY VS. UNHEALTHY DOUBT

Doubt, as I've come to understand it, can be broken down into two very disparate, well-defined categories: doubt based on intellect and doubt based on fear. Unfortunately, the latter can often disguise itself as the former, making the distinctions between the two important to understand.

Intellect-Based Doubt

Intellect-based doubt is what some might call "healthy doubt." It stems from our innate inquisitiveness and natural inclination to challenge the apparent, and it fuels our human curiosity and caution. It is based on reason, logic, and rational deduction. And it most definitely serves us well.

Consider some of the great scientists — Albert Einstein, Galileo, Copernicus, Charles Darwin; the great philosophers — Socrates, Plato, René Descartes, Saint Augustine; and the great revolutionaries — Thomas Jefferson, Abraham Lincoln, Mohandas Gandhi, Martin Luther King Jr. All employed their intellect-based doubt to challenge the accepted but flawed paradigms of their time, and all changed the world in very positive ways.

And what about the great spiritual believers — those individuals who have shaped our religious and spiritual frameworks? They too, I would argue, were some of the greatest doubters who ever lived. Historian Jennifer Michael Hecht does a masterful job of making sense of this paradox in her bestseller *Doubt: A History*, tracing a religious and philosophical evolution and showing how each generation's doubt becomes the next generation's certainty.

Most of us are not actively seeking to challenge paradigms or change the world. We are, however, trying to navigate through life; and for that task, we too need to draw on our intellect-based doubt and act *with* it, again and again.

ON HEALTHY DOUBT

Jennifer Michael Hecht, PhD, author of *Doubt: A History*

Q: I've heard you say that history's greatest doubters and greatest believers have a lot in common. Can you explain?

A: What I'm suggesting is that the great doubters are more like the great believers than the great mass of people. They're both deeply entrenched in questions and thinking about issues. And so the people who are putting forward opposing positions are really on the same team in comparison to all the people who don't care.

Q: These individuals you've profiled in *Doubt* — the great doubters — what is their common thread? What is the one thing you can point to in all these people?

A: Most of the great doubters constructively use their doubt. Most of them decide that — because of their doubt — they have to help other people. As in Plato's parable of the cave, they're always going back down into the cave to help drag

continued ➭

5

more people up into the sun, even though the sun hurts. It occurs to me that this parable is very interesting for someone with OCD, because you have to drag a person up into the very painful light of the day, but once they get there they realize that that's truth, not what they were playing in the dark of the cave. It's a real beauty. It shows you that learning always hurts. If you're not hurting, you're not learning; you're just adding some facts to your old picture of the world.

Q: **What can the average person draw from your research into the historical role of healthy doubt?**

A: The answer is joy. Joy. The welcoming into your whole self of a "not-knowing" is a profound opportunity. You get a profound sense of joy in trying to figure out the world and be creative and loving within this absurd universe. It creates in people a feeling of sudden freedom. So often people describe accepting doubt into their lives as [deciding] that they're not going to close down into some new certainty. To use a metaphor I see all the time through history, it's like suddenly being let out into a field to just run and be.

Fear-Based Doubt

I happen to be sitting in a Starbucks in New York City at this moment, watching a man outside my window contemplating the wisdom of crossing Park Avenue against the flashing "Don't Walk" light, as the woman in front of him has just done. He takes a step off the curb, only to hesitate and return to the sidewalk. Clearly, his intellect-based doubt has left him questioning his ability to cross the four lanes of traffic without getting run over.

In this case, reason, logic, and rational deduction have served this pedestrian well. But what if my guy on the street corner (I'll call him Fred) decides he should never cross Park Avenue? Maybe he recalls a recent news story about a pedestrian killed in a Manhattan crosswalk and worries that he'll be next. He thinks back on the countless times he has crossed this street. He's never been hit. He's never seen anyone else get hit. But still Fred stands there, frozen by fear. *What if he gets crushed by a speeding car? What if he's killed? Who will take care of his family?* A knot grows in his stomach. He feels his heart race.

Is this intellect-based doubt that's keeping Fred on the corner?

No. This, I would venture to say, is an "unhealthy" form of doubt we all battle to some degree — namely, fear-based doubt, or uncertainty based not on reason, logic, and rational deduction but rather on emotional, black-and-white, and catastrophic thinking. Fred knows at some intellectual level that the odds of his getting hit crossing Park Avenue with the light are infinitesimal. Yet he is allowing his fear to suggest that because someone has been killed in this fashion, he could — and likely, would — be as well; and that prospect is unacceptable.

Fortunately, as I continue to ponder all this, the "Walk" light turns green for Fred, and he makes his way safely across Park Avenue and out of my view. From here, I imagine, he will continue using his intellect-based doubt to navigate his way across one Manhattan street after another to wherever it is he's going.

ON HEALTHY VS. UNHEALTHY DOUBT

Stephen Hinshaw, PhD, Professor and Chair,
Department of Psychology, University of California, Berkeley

Q: Why do we need intellect-based doubt?
A: Well, the world as we all know it isn't the most predictable place. There is poverty; there is, as we now know today,

continued ⤵

huge economic uncertainty. There are problems that we all face in terms of knowing what the right thing to do is. So we had better have, for lack of a better term, rational doubt about what we should be doing with our lives, because there are so many decisions to be made every minute, every hour, every day.

Q: **What about fear-based doubt: why does this form of doubt tend to impact us in unhealthy ways?**

A: What happens is that such fear-based doubt kicks in lots of physiological responses. If I'm really engaging in this fear-based doubt, I am probably secreting cortisol, a stress hormone, throughout my body, because cortisol is one of the hormones that prepares us to fight or flee. It's really good that that happens when an elephant or some other predator comes charging into the room; but what if we're secreting cortisol and other stress hormones when we don't need to be? We now know, from fifty years of research, that there are real physiological and psychological consequences of being in this stressed state. This sets the stage for diabetes. This sets the stage for coronary artery disease and stroke, especially if you have other underlying vulnerabilities. It is also clearly implicated in the affective disorder known as depression. In other words, if my body is not going to use the cortisol and stress hormones and take that energy surge, there's nothing to do with it, and it's going to take a physiological and psychological toll in terms of some of our leading killer diseases and in terms of things like depression.

Q: **Is it human nature for us to try to rid ourselves of the discomfort that stems from doubt?**

A: It is human nature, a lot of psychologists have said, to be in a state of equilibrium. We resist, at a bodily level, terribly

continued ⤳

uncomfortable feelings. And we'll do almost anything to kind of right ourselves — to be out of this plagued mental feeling and out of this stress-hormone-laden physiological burden.

The Fuzzy Lines of the Shadow

Fred chose to cross the street, acting *with* doubt. Had he opted not to, he might have instead crossed a threshold from intellect- to fear-based doubt, from a New York street corner to the Shadow of Doubt. Maybe he would have stayed in the Shadow only for the duration of a traffic-light cycle, coming to his senses quickly and getting on with his life. But maybe he would have remained stuck *within* doubt, like so many of the people I'll introduce you to in the pages ahead. And maybe Fred would have been none the wiser about why he made the choices he did.

The truth is, there are no gates at the edge of the Shadow, no clear signs to welcome us or let us know when we're leaving. Guideposts would be very helpful, indeed. But they don't exist. Instead, most of us have to figure out for ourselves when we have slipped into the realm of fear-based doubt, and that's often no easy task. As I warned, the same fear-based doubt that can distort our thinking is also quite adept at masquerading as intellect-based doubt.

So how then do we know when our doubts are healthy and deserve our attention? How do we know when they are fear-based and distorting our thinking? Allow me to take a stab at answering those questions with a series of other questions I've learned to ask.

- Does this doubt evoke far more anxiety than either curiosity or prudent caution?
- Does this doubt pose a series of increasingly distressing "what if" questions?

- Does this doubt stem from logic-defying and/or black-and-white assumptions?
- Does this doubt prompt a strong urge to act — or avoid acting — in a fashion others might perceive as excessive, in order to reduce the anxiety it creates?

And, last but certainly not least:

- Would you be embarrassed or frightened to explain your "what if" questions to a police officer or work supervisor?

If you answer Yes to these five questions, the chances are pretty good that your vantage point is somewhere within the Shadow of Doubt. That, at least, has been my experience, again and again — with one critical caveat, which I'll explain shortly. First, though, let's plop Fred back on the corner as he ponders whether he has enough time to cross the street against the flashing "Don't Walk" light, and see if we can answer my five questions for him.

Q: **Does this doubt evoke far more anxiety than either curiosity or prudent caution?**

A: Probably not. Fred's reasonable uncertainty may make him somewhat anxious, but probably not more anxious than cautious.

Q: **Does this doubt pose a series of increasingly distressing "what if" questions?**

A: Not necessarily. Although Fred may be concerned that he might not make it across the street in time, that doesn't mean he necessarily starts pondering his imminent death and its consequences. He may instead wonder if he'll hold up traffic, get stuck on the center divider, or have to dash back to the curb.

Q: **Does this doubt stem from logic-defying and/or black-and-white assumptions?**

A: No. Fred's reasoning is based on fairly logical assumptions about how long he has to cross the street and whether he might be hit — a serious but not certain possibility.

Q: Does this doubt prompt a strong urge to act — or avoid acting — in a fashion others might see as excessive, in order to reduce the anxiety it creates?

A: No. Fred's doubt prompts him to step back to the curb (and avoid crossing the street), an action unlikely to be seen as excessive by anyone around him.

Q: Would Fred be embarrassed or frightened to explain his "what if" questions to a police officer or work supervisor?

A: I wouldn't think so. I imagine a cop would probably tell him it was wise to consider his timing.

If we look strictly at my screening criteria, then, we can rule out fear-based doubt as the source of Fred's concern and instead credit Fred with using good judgment and acting *with* doubt. Attaboy, Fred!

But now, how about my hypothetical Fred, the one paralyzed by a fear of getting run over, even crossing with the light, because he's read about someone who was hit? We'll ask the same five questions:

Q: Does this doubt evoke far more anxiety than either curiosity or prudent caution?

A: Yes. Fred feels his heart racing and his gut tightening as he ponders his demise, even before he considers any prudent alternative actions.

Q: Does this doubt pose a series of increasingly distressing "what if" questions?

A: Yes. Fred quickly moves from *What if I get hit?* to *What if I die?* to *What if I'm not around to take care of my family and they can't get by without me?*

Q: Does this doubt stem from logic-defying and/or black-and-white assumptions?

A: Yes. Fred reasons that because someone else died in a freak accident while crossing a New York street legally, he likely will too. His assumptions are both illogical and black-and-white.

Q: Does this doubt prompt a strong urge to act — or avoid acting — in a fashion others might see as excessive, in order to reduce the anxiety it creates?

A: Yes. Fred's doubt prompts a strong urge to avoid crossing the street, not just on the "Don't Walk" light, but ever. Excessive? Yes!

Q: Would Fred be embarrassed or frightened to explain his "what if" questions to a police officer or work supervisor?

A: Yes. I'm fairly certain my imaginary friend would feel pretty silly explaining to a cop that he's afraid he won't ever survive crossing the street, even with the light.

Five for five. Hypothetical Fred, we can safely conclude, is a victim of fear-based doubt; he is indeed trapped within the Shadow of Doubt. Sorry, big guy.

Back now to that little caveat I put on my screening questions and their ability to ferret out fear-based doubt. They work. They really do. I've employed them countless times to help others see the distortions of their unhealthy "what if" questions. But, truth be told, I'm afraid that when attempting to use these questions (or any others) to help me identify my own fear-based doubt, I've often found them, well, worthless.

As Albert Einstein is said to have remarked, "Problems cannot be solved at the same level of awareness that created them," and there's the rub. Trying to recognize the distortions of fear-based doubt while under the control of fear-based doubt is next to impossible. This is the challenge facing those of us who have found ourselves lost in the

Shadow of Doubt, where logic and reason are as scarce as shade trees in a desert.

And here's one more twist: fear, whatever its source, generates a real physiological response by which we gauge risk. Whether prompted by the sudden appearance of a man pointing a gun at you or some ridiculous "what if" question in your head, the feeling is identical. So, as bestselling author David Burns likes to point out, "emotional reasoning" can lead to all kinds of confusion and trouble. It works like this: the thought of crossing the street makes me *feel* very anxious, therefore the risk, I reason, must *be* very real.

ON EMOTIONAL REASONING

David Burns, MD, author of *When Panic Attacks*

Q: Sometimes even my most ridiculous fears feel very real... and that somehow seems to give credence to the triggers behind them.

A: Absolutely. We often feel convinced that we're in danger when we're really not.

Q: Is this what you refer to as "emotional reasoning"?

A: Yes. Emotional reasoning is a term I coined, and it's one of the ten distorted thinking patterns that trigger anxiety as well as depression. Emotional reasoning means that you reason from how you feel. You tell yourself, "I *feel* afraid, so I must *be* in danger." For example, if you have the fear of flying, and you have to get on a plane, you may tell yourself, "Wow, I'm really terrified. Flying must be incredibly dangerous. What if the plane runs into turbulence and crashes?"

Depressed individuals also engage in emotional reasoning, but it's a little different. They tell themselves, "I *feel*

continued ⮧

worthless, therefore I must *be* worthless." Or "I *feel* hopeless, therefore it must be a fact that I'll never get better." Then, after they recover and feel joy and self-esteem again, they can see how irrational those thoughts were.

Emotional reasoning is highly misleading because our feelings always result from our thoughts, and never from reality. This idea goes all the way back to Epictetus nearly two thousand years ago. In his famous *Enchiridion*, he said that people are disturbed not by things, but by the views we take of them — in other words, our thoughts. And if our thoughts are distorted and illogical, then our emotions will not reflect reality any more than those funny mirrors in amusement parks that make us look grotesque.

Sometimes positive emotions can be way off base, too. Did you ever go to Las Vegas and put a quarter in the slot machine and tell yourself, "I really think I'm going to earn the eight-million-dollar jackpot this time? I can just *feel* it in my bones." Did you ever have that feeling?

Q: Oh, sure.

A: How many times did you actually win the eight-million-dollar jackpot?

Q: I'm afraid it hasn't happened yet.

A: Yeah, exactly. That's the whole problem with emotional reasoning. It's not always a bad thing, because sometimes our negative emotions protect us from real danger. But healthy fear, of course, is radically different from neurotic anxiety, or a phobia.

Q: And for those of us with extreme fear-based doubts, emotional reasoning can certainly feed our vicious cycles, can't it?

A: Absolutely.

The more I've learned to manage my OCD, the more I've been able to use my screening questions to help me recognize when I'm stuck in Doubt. They have served me well in this sense, and I share them with you as a tool for sorting out what's what in the world of doubt. But the real process of making belief, by necessity, transcends mere logic, a faculty that I think you'll soon understand is often not available to those of us with the doubting disease.

KEY POINTS

- Almost everyone faces two distinct forms of doubt:
  - ✳ Intellect-based (or healthy) doubt.
  - ✳ Fear-based (or unhealthy) doubt.
- Intellect-based doubt can be characterized as follows:
  - ✳ It's based on reason, logic, and rational deduction.
  - ✳ It tends to prompt curiosity and/or caution.
  - ✳ It leads us to act *with* doubt in a constructive way.
- Fear-based doubt can be characterized as follows:
  - ✳ It's based on illogical and/or black-and-white assumptions.
  - ✳ It tends to spike our anxiety.
  - ✳ It leads to increasingly distressing "what if" questions.
  - ✳ It compels us to act — or avoid acting — in a fashion others might find excessive in order to reduce the anxiety it creates.
  - ✳ It ultimately leaves us stuck *within* doubt.
- Recognizing fear-based doubt can be difficult because:
  - ✳ It often masks itself as intellect-based doubt.
  - ✳ Emotional reasoning gives us false evidence that the anxiety stemming from our fear-based doubts is warranted: "I feel anxious, therefore the source of my anxiety must be a legitimate concern."

CHAPTER TWO

Octopuses Chewing Doubt-nuts

An Introduction to OCD

M any years ago, when I was writing my first book and my daughters were still too young to understand the nature of Daddy's challenges, they came up with their own definition for the "OCD" acronym they'd seen on the pages scattered across my desk: "Octopuses Chewing Doughnuts."

Little did they know what a precious gift they'd given me with their fertile imaginations. Little did I know how much I would draw on that particular image to understand the mechanics of OCD and the nature of those tricky creatures who troll the Shadow of Doubt. Although somewhere along the way *doughnuts* morphed into *doubt-nuts*, my daughters' original OCD definition remains my favorite to this day. Of course, to fully understand the "octopuses," the "doubt-nuts," and the "chewing" process, we may need some slightly more scientific definitions.

OCD BASICS

Numerous terrific books have been written about this disorder known as the "doubting disease," many of which I will point you toward in the pages ahead. Because the intent of this book is to explore only those aspects of OCD that offer insight into the mechanics and impacts of fear-based doubt, I will limit my overview of OCD here to a quick one and encourage you to focus on those themes common to both OCD and everyday, fear-based doubt — namely, emotion-driven, black-and-white, often catastrophic thinking rooted in the past and future and accompanied by compelling urges to alleviate discomfort.

Clinically speaking, obsessive compulsive disorder is an anxiety disorder marked by intrusive, unwanted thoughts and repeated actions or rituals aimed at dislodging these thoughts. It is believed to affect at least one in every one hundred adults, and men and women in roughly equal measure. The disorder can set in at any point from preschool to adulthood, and far too often it goes unrecognized. In fact, studies suggest it takes people with OCD an average of fourteen to seventeen years (from the time their OCD begins) to get the treatment they need. Although OCD can be both chronic and debilitating, it is also highly treatable.

Most scientists believe the roots of OCD are biochemical and involve communication problems between distinct parts of the brain, specifically the orbital cortex and the basal ganglia. Studies also suggest that the neurotransmitter serotonin plays a key role in the communication breakdown. Beyond that, honestly, I get lost in all the mumbo jumbo of unpronounceable neurological terms and complex physiological explanations. I do know that the experts all agree on one thing: the OCD brain is different from the non-OCD brain, both structurally and functionally. And, thanks to recent advances in brain imaging, they can now effectively prove that theory.

ON OCD BRAIN IMAGING

Michael Jenike, MD, Professor of Psychiatry, Harvard Medical School; Chair, OC Foundation Scientific Advisory Board

Q: **In general terms, how does brain imaging work?**

A: Neuroimaging uses various techniques to look at either the structure of the brain or the function of the brain. For example, magnetic resonance imaging (MRI) allows researchers to view the actual structure of the brain. Positron emission tomography (PET) and functional MRI (fMRI) allow them to view the functioning of the brain and tell what part of the brain is active during specific activities. These techniques can be used to compare patients with OCD to normal controls to determine differences in [brain] structure or functioning.

Q: **In what ways does the OCD brain look different from non-OCD brains?**

A: In OCD research, we have scans to compare brain structure in OCD patients versus normal controls, and OCD patients have more gray matter and less white matter in the brain. Functional scans, meantime, have shown increased activity in the orbital frontal areas (above the eyes) in OCD patients. Also, they have been used to show that the abnormal activity becomes closer to normal as patients get better through either behavior therapy or medication.

Q: **What does this tell us about the mechanics of OCD?**

A: It tells us that OCD involves circuits in the brain, as well as specific brain areas. There are also subtle structural differences. It's hard to say what this all means at this time; but as

continued ↴

we gain a better understanding of the anatomy and functioning of the OCD brain, it will likely help us in terms of new treatments.

THE ENDLESS LOOP

Outwardly, OCD manifests itself in a wide variety of ways, marked by various combinations of well-defined obsessions and compulsions (as described below). It would be easy to conclude that the disorder presents a number of very different challenges, both for sufferers and those who treat them; but in fact all of OCD's "flavors" have the same vicious cycle at their core. My favorite description of this cycle is one introduced by Drs. Edna Foa and Reid Wilson in their book *Stop Obsessing* and elaborated on by Dr. Tamar Chansky in her book *Freeing Your Child from Obsessive-Compulsive Disorder*. As they define it, this cycle is made up of four components: obsessions, distress, compulsions, and relief.

Obsessions

Ever get a song stuck in your head? It plays again and again, looping in your brain like a skipping record. Over and over, the words repeat themselves, perhaps amusing you at first, but then distracting you, then frustrating you, and ultimately annoying the heck out of you.

Here, allow me to refresh your memory:

Jingle bells, jingle bells . . .
Jingle all the way . . .

Can you hear the words looping?

Jingle . . . bells . . . jingle . . . bells . . .
Jingle . . . all . . . the . . . way . . .

And, if that didn't work, try a few lines of "It's a Small World After All." (Yes, I know you're going to be cursing me very shortly.)

Okay, now imagine that the lyrics you're "hearing," however loud and intrusive they may seem to you at this moment, are in fact a hundred times louder, a hundred times more resonant, and a hundred times more all-consuming.

Next, imagine that the words bouncing around in your head have been doing so for hours, not minutes.

And finally, imagine that, instead of representing the lyrics of some silly song, the words looping in your head are actually those of a question beginning with "what if" and ending with one of the most horrific consequences you can imagine.

What if I ran over someone? What if I ran over someone? What if I . . .
What if these germs kill me? What if these germs kill me? What if these germs . . .
What if my thoughts send me to hell? What if my thoughts send me to hell? What if my thoughts . . .

This, I'm afraid, is about as close as I can get you to an OCD obsession, and I know that my analogy falls short. I also know that offering up an example like this is somewhat akin to describing an elephant based solely on what it looks and feels like standing next to only its tail or trunk. In reality, OCD obsessions take on many forms. Some seem almost audible, much like the endlessly repeating songs I've described above. Others, however, are more visual in nature and take the form of vivid images or looping image sequences. Their focus might involve contamination, harm to others, hypermorality, or excessive concern about symmetry (just to name a few common issues), and their triggers can range from the mundane to the ridiculous.

What all obsessions share are these key hallmarks: they are intrusive, involuntary, distracting, disturbing, irrational, and, most of all, distressing.

Distress

If describing the intrusive nature of obsessions is difficult, then conveying the distress they create is next to impossible. In fact, I'd guess this particular challenge represents the single greatest frustration most people with OCD have when trying to explain their disorder to others. And without an understanding of the distress created by our obsessions, who could possibly understand our seeming inability to curb our compulsions?

So, then, what's so distressing about obsessions?

First, they are often ugly. Really, really ugly. For many of us, they are the very worst "what if " questions we can ask, representing our deepest fears. It's almost as if each of us has an internal doubt bully (the Octopus, if you will) who knows how to push our most anxiety-provoking buttons. For me, that button reads "Harm" and prompts this recurring question: *What if I, through my negligence, unknowingly harmed or might harm someone or something?* This is the "what if " question at the core of virtually all my obsessions: *What if that pothole I ran over was actually a body, and someone is lying in the street bleeding? What if I unknowingly bumped into some kid in the crowded mall, perhaps giving him a concussion that will ruin his life?* My "Harm" button spikes my anxiety like no other and quickly leads to vivid obsessions about the horrors I have undoubtedly inflicted. My bully, knowing this, finds every possible opportunity to push that button.

While the fear of doing harm is a fairly common focus of OCD obsessions, it is only one of many. For some sufferers, the core fear is getting sick, and their bullies push buttons reading "Germs" that lead to questions such as *What if I touch that doorknob after someone with AIDS has used it?* For them, such questions quickly lead to obsessions about falling deathly ill or dying. (Never mind that they know that AIDS cannot be spread in such a fashion.)

As ugly as these core questions themselves might be, I doubt they'd be so distressing without the power of neurochemistry behind them. And for this, we with OCD can thank our amygdalas and the chemical releases for which they're responsible. Again deferring to the brain scientists to explain the mechanics of all this, I've come to understand the process as a twist on the evolutionary "fight or flight" responses prompted by human fear.

Let's say a bear storms into your room right now. It growls, bares its teeth, and thrusts its front paws toward you, as if to attack. You, without even thinking, react in one of two ways: either you run as fast and as far away as you can, or you ready yourself for a fight. This is the way evolution has conditioned humans to respond to threats, and it has certainly saved us from a lot of bear attacks over the millennia.

But here's the catch for those of us with OCD: We don't need a bear or a lion — or any other legitimate threat — to trigger our fight-or-flight responses. Our core fears — those "what if " questions our bullies pose — do the trick just fine. With one simple push of our anxiety buttons, our bullies activate chemical responses in our amygdalas, which in turn trigger fight-or-flight reactions.

Because the biochemical process behind this response is identical regardless of the trigger, the anxiety we OCD sufferers feel (from, say, touching a doorknob) is every bit as powerful as what you might feel if that bear really did burst into your room. And, as described in chapter 1, we are left battling what psychologists term "emotional reasoning." Yeah, we know — at least at some intellectual level — that catching AIDS from a doorknob is not possible. But because the fear feels so real, it suggests to us that perhaps our anxiety is, in fact, warranted. Another weapon for the bully.

And here is the bully's final weapon: in the thick of OCD distress, many of us become convinced we might be left battling it forever. *Gotcha!* my bully will taunt. *What if you will have to live with this discomfort for the rest of your life?*

That, for me, is the ultimate "what if " question!

In an attempt to convey the distress OCD can create, I want to share a story with you now that I've never before put into print. In fact, I believe it's the only personal story I've ever held back on sharing in my OCD outreach, because for years I could never acknowledge the shame that it caused me.

It's early 1995, and I have just received a phone message from my wife, Samantha, sounding as distraught as I've ever heard her. "I'm in an ambulance with Brianna," her breathy voicemail starts. "Meet me in the emergency room at Mills Hospital." And that's it. No other details. For all I know, my one-year-old daughter is dying.

I jump in my car and, despite my OCD obsessions about unknowingly running someone over, I head for the hospital as quickly as I can. Images of a bloodied, blue-faced Brianna fill my mind as I navigate the busy streets, breaking speed limits and otherwise standing up to my "follow the rules" bully. Nothing will keep me from getting to my precious baby in her time of need.

But then, less than a block from the hospital, as I make a sharp right turn, I hear a loud thud beneath my car. Kuhhh-LANK! Without even thinking, I slow to a stop and try to come up with an explanation for the noise. A soda can? A stray battery? A rock kicked up by my tires? I know what's next — the all too predictable questions my bully is ready to ask:

What if that was someone you ran over, Jeff?

What if some poor kid is hobbling away right now as you sit here in the car?

What if you never know what happened?

Crap! I'm doomed.

Just down the street, my daughter lies on an emergency-room gurney, doctors hovering around her as they treat her for God knows what. Perhaps she will draw her last breath before I can get there. And here I am, paralyzed by doubt in my car as the precious seconds tick away.

Compulsions

The distress I was battling at that moment was unbearable. Literally. Sitting there in my car, I wanted, needed, even craved relief. With every fiber of my being I longed to turn the car around and head in search of evidence that might exonerate me.

In the end, I didn't. The pull of my potentially dying child ultimately proved more powerful than that of my doubt bully — if only slightly. I made it to the emergency room, where I discovered that Brianna had suffered only a febrile seizure and would be just fine.

Unfortunately, this was one of the very few times during this stretch of my life that I successfully stood up to my bully. And I did it only because of a life-or-death situation. Most days, time and again, I gave in to my relief-offering urges — urges that led me to actions known in the OCD world as compulsions.

As with obsessions, compulsions take a wide variety of forms, including checking, washing, ordering, counting, repeating, and hoarding. What they share is their recurring, ritualistic nature and their ability to provide temporary relief from their associated obsessions.

Driving back to check on the source of the clank that triggered my obsessive "what if" questions was a compulsion in that it offered me a temporary reprieve from OCD distress. As someone with harm obsessions, I myself am highly prone to checking. For the guy concerned about catching AIDS from the doorknob, the enticing compulsion is to wash his hands. For both of us, yielding to our compulsive urges gives us temporary relief.

In my outreach talks, I have found that most non-OCD audiences can relate, at least at some level, to checking and washing compulsions. They too have checked their stoves and doors. They too have scrubbed their hands after touching something especially icky. But when I share stories about my friends who address their obsessions by repeating motions, such as flipping a light switch on and off three times, or those who have to arrange items in a certain fashion to find relief from their obsessions, I tend to see a lot of raised eyebrows. I imagine many in the audience are asking themselves, Is this really the same destructive OCD cycle at work?

It is. OCD, at its core, is about faulty brain wiring: The intrusive thought — let's call it Obsession O — is frightening and triggers unbearable anxiety. The compulsive action — let's call it Compulsion C — has helped me (temporarily) reduce my anxiety about O in the past. Therefore, my brain reasons, I should do C again to find this relief. When it comes right down to it, the specific nature of the Os and Cs (that is, the thoughts and actions) is not all that relevant.

I actually learned this lesson the hard way. Early on in my therapy, I remember shaking my head at the absurdity of the handwashing compulsions a friend was describing. Because contamination fears were not among my own obsessions, I couldn't imagine why anyone could get stuck at a sink scrubbing her hands over and over. My checking compulsions, of course, were much more logical. (Not!)

Years later, though, while reporting on an outbreak of hepatitis, I learned from a county health official that the problem had started with "a single pair of unsanitary hands." *Gotcha!* I could almost hear my bully taunting.

From that moment on, I faced a whole new slew of harm obsessions, a whole new bevy of "what if" questions about the potential of my own hands to cause outbreaks of some horrific plague. These obsessions quickly led to washing compulsions, and the more I indulged them, the more I connected my new O with my new C. Before I knew it I was a bona fide washer, much like those "freaks" I'd laughed at years before.

I imagine my friends with ordering and repeating compulsions developed their cycles in much the same way. At some point, they probably found that flipping a light switch on and off three times, or arranging their socks in some particular fashion, helped them (temporarily) reduce their anxiety in ways that even they didn't understand. The more they repeated the ritual, the deeper a neural groove developed between their Os and Cs.

Relief

I've never battled any kind of chemical addiction. Through my outreach over the past couple of years, though, I have met and gotten to know many people who have. I think we fascinate each other, largely because of the parallels between our battles, especially when it comes to the power of our cravings and the destructive ways in which we indulge them.

The two disorders are very different, of course, with alcoholism typically centered on a positive reinforcement (the "high" or buzz), and OCD centered exclusively on a negative reinforcement (distress prompting a desire for relief). Still, I've come to believe that the relief we with OCD get from our compulsions is every bit as intense as the rush experienced by alcoholics and addicts through their use of booze and drugs. In both cases, that payoff is immediate, overwhelmingly powerful, and short-lived.

When I am deep in the Shadow of Doubt, clawing my way along its edges and searching for a quick escape, I am very much a junkie in search of a fix. And the relief I feel when I find it is, I imagine, of the same order as the payoff an alcoholic gets when he downs a shot of whiskey, or an addict gets when she shoots heroin into her veins.

Ahhhhhhhhhhhhhhhhhhhhhh.

Unfortunately, as with any vicious cycle, the more I found relief through my compulsive fixes, the more I turned to them again and again. Much as my recovering alcoholic friends tell me that one drink was never enough, for me, one check of the door or one scrubbing of my hands was never enough.

Obsession. Distress. Compulsion. Relief.
Obsession. Distress. Compulsion. Relief.
Obsession. Distress. Compulsion . . .

THE OCTOPUS REVISITED

OCD therapists often encourage clients to externalize their disorder — that is, to think of the source of their obsessions and compulsions as some force or creature separate from themselves. The objective, as I've always understood it, is twofold: first, to help OCD sufferers understand that they are not merely composites of the thoughts that plague them; and second, to define the disorder as an entity that people with OCD can stand up to and fight back against. I'm a big fan of this approach and have seen both kids and adults benefit from it greatly.

In my own recovery, I have come to think of my bully as a figure called Director Doubt, and I'll say more about him later. In the early days, though, it was my daughters' doubt-nut-chewing octopus (whom they affectionately named Octi) who played the role of my nemesis. And I can think of no better way to summarize the mechanics of OCD than to offer you a "screenplay" of Octi in action during my worst years.

SCENE 1: We see Octi looking hungry. He survives on doubt-nuts (my compulsions), and he needs me to feed them to him by performing my rituals.

SCENE 2: To get me to feed him, Octi must first trigger my obsessions by pushing my "Harm" button. He starts posing "what if" questions until one of them does the trick. Let's say he gets me with the question *What if you didn't set your parking brake?*

SCENE 3: Knowing he has me now, Octi begins suggesting a number of actions I can take that will offer me relief (and feed him in the process). *Perhaps you should go back to your car and check the brake*, he suggests.

SCENE 4: Octi knows I don't want to indulge my compulsive urges, so he steps up the pressure, posing increasingly disturbing questions, such as *What if the car rolls away and crushes someone?*

SCENE 5: I give up and return to my car to check on the brake. In so doing, I feed Octi a doubt-nut.

SCENE 6: Octi chews his doubt-nut. He grows stronger. So does his appetite. He gets hungry again, even hungrier than last time. He needs me to feed him again . . .

Standing up to our Octi's. Seeing them for what they are. Choosing not to feed them doubt-nuts. These, I'm convinced, are the keys not only to fighting OCD, but also — as I hope to show in part 2 of this book — to *making belief* any time we're stuck in doubt.

So how have those of us recovering from OCD learned to do this? The short answer is cognitive behavior therapy.

ON OCD DISTRESS

Tamar Chansky, PhD, author of
Freeing Your Child from Obsessive-Compulsive Disorder

Q: You write that we are drawn to that which rescues us. What do you mean by this?

A: The brain is trying to protect us at all times and do the best that it can. Sometimes what happens — as with OCD — is

continued

---

that the brain warns us about things that we don't need to be worried about. But what we feel is that we're really in danger. So of course if there's a strategy, a way to relieve that danger and that very uncomfortable feeling, we're going to adopt that method and stay pretty close to it.

Q: In explaining why it's so difficult to break out of this cycle, you liken compulsions to mosquito bites.

A: When working with children, initially that's a very helpful way to talk about the process because basically the more that you scratch a mosquito bite, the more you feel you need to do it, and that's really what kids and adults can learn when it comes to OCD compulsions: the more you do them, the harder it becomes to stop. But they can also learn to resist itching for short periods of time, and see how they are in control.

Q: You use a lot of metaphors in your work with kids. Talk, if you would, about the "helpful neighbor" metaphor for compulsions.

A: OCD is like a helpful, albeit intrusive, neighbor that you really don't like. So let's say you get lost when you are driving, and — feeling stranded and confused — you stop by the side of the road, and a neighbor you just don't like comes to help you; you feel indebted to that person because they have helped you. Meantime, that person may expect more and more from you to sort of repay that big favor, saying, "I saved you!" when actually you surely would have figured it out yourself; and then it becomes a vicious cycle that you need to keep. But the fact is that you were never stranded in the first place, so they didn't do you any favor. That's really what OCD treatment is all about: realizing that, despite the risk you perceive, you actually weren't in danger in the first place. You're not stranded at all; you're just having a bad thought.

OCD TREATMENT

Generally speaking, OCD is best treated with some form of cognitive behavior therapy (CBT), often in combination with prescribed medication. While the topic of pharmacotherapy is certainly important, it exceeds the scope of this book. Because of that, I encourage those of you seeking OCD treatment information to read the latest research regarding medication, available through a variety of resources, including the OC Foundation website (www.ocfoundation.org). Here, I want to focus on CBT and the lessons it can offer all of us — with or without OCD.

As its name suggests, cognitive behavior therapy aims to address both problematic cognitions (thinking patterns) and counterproductive behaviors. There are probably as many distinct combinations of these two aspects of CBT today as there are CBT therapists, and there is ongoing debate as to where the optimal balance lies.

My personal conclusion, based on my own experience and the recoveries of people I've observed through my outreach — along with a growing body of scientific evidence — is that the most effective form of CBT is a behavior-based one known as exposure/response-prevention, or ERP. (ERP as CBT for OCD...this chapter is starting to look like one of my teen daughters' text messages!)

ERP is essentially a structured desensitization process designed to help people with OCD gradually and systematically face down their fears. By exposing OCD clients to their triggers and preventing them from carrying out their associated compulsive responses, therapists help their clients see that when they sit with their anxiety, that anxiety will diminish, even without their performing the compulsions.

Dr. Chansky likens the process to jumping into a cold swimming pool. If you stay in it long enough, that jarring, icy feeling passes — not because the water has warmed up, but because your brain has stopped paying attention to the message "It's cold, it's cold!" You habituate yourself to the water. Similarly, Chansky argues, people with OCD can habituate themselves to their anxiety by sitting with it long enough for their brains to stop sending out a "Danger, danger!" message.

All of this is far easier said than done — both for OCD therapists and their clients. For the process to be effective, therapists must work with clients to develop exposure hierarchies with progressively (but not prohibitively) difficult challenges. If, for example, the client obsesses about getting sick from other people's germs and compulsively avoids situations that his bully suggests could contaminate him, the therapist might have the client identify a number of potential triggers — from touching a doorknob to sitting in a theater to visiting a hospital — and rank them based on the anxiety that each scenario evokes. Together, they could then design a sequence of exposure exercises, starting with the least anxiety-provoking challenges and working up the hierarchy to tougher ones. Sometimes, of necessity, this process also involves imaginary exposures — certainly when real-life ones (such as running someone over) are impractical, impossible, or, well, immoral.

I speak from firsthand experience when I say that ERP is tough work. Really tough work. And there are no shortcuts; I know, because I looked for them. Still, the rewards are immeasurable.

At its crux, OCD treatment is about learning to live with the discomfort of uncertainty. In the chapters that follow, I aim to show that the same is true about life.

KEY POINTS

- OCD is an anxiety disorder marked by intrusive unwanted thoughts (obsessions) and repeated actions or rituals (compulsions) aimed at dislodging these thoughts.

- OCD is thought to affect at least one in one hundred adults.
- Although the precise cause of OCD remains unknown, scientists believe it is biochemical in nature.
- OCD can be chronic but is also highly treatable.
- The OCD cycle is made up of four parts:
  * Obsessions
  * Distress
  * Compulsions
  * Relief
- OCD is typically best treated with cognitive behavior therapy (CBT), often combined with medication.
- A technique called exposure/response-prevention (ERP) is at the core of CBT treatment for OCD.
  * ERP therapy aims to systematically desensitize OCD sufferers to their anxiety by having them sit with that anxiety.
  * For ERP to be effective, therapists and clients must develop hierarchies of increasingly difficult exposure challenges.

CHAPTER THREE

Trapdoors

False Exits When Stuck in Doubt

L et's take a tour.

I want to show you around the Shadow of Doubt — its border areas, familiar to many, and its deepest, darkest corners, known only by those of us who stumble into them because of our faulty brain chemistry. Mostly, I want to point out its trapdoors, those apparent escape routes that only take us deeper into the darkness. To this end, I have enlisted the help of a number of tour guides. Some of them are card-carrying members of the Recovering Obsessive Compulsives Club (imagine what that secret handshake looks like!); others are friends and colleagues who, although they do not have OCD, have found themselves battling uncertainty to one degree or another in their lives.

Because I am dressing all my guides in the same uniforms, so to speak, I need to reiterate what might otherwise be lost just above: some of the misadventures in doubt I'm about to share are the result of OCD, some are not. I've chosen to include both kinds here to draw parallels, *not* to suggest that everyone "has a touch of OCD" (an all too common misconception). OCD is a specific biochemical brain disorder with specific diagnostic criteria and mechanics. It is not a condition people slip into and out of. The challenges and discomfort it presents typically far exceed those of everyday, fear-based doubt.

My intent in this chapter is to highlight several parallels between OCD and fear-based doubt, and specifically the counterproductive ways in which we tend to address the discomfort of both. So, although the circumstances that have led my tour guides and me into the Shadow of Doubt may be very different, our distorted decision making once inside ("in Doubt," if you will), has led all of us to a common set of trapdoors.

TRAPDOOR 1: CHECKING

Locks. Doors. Appliances. Envelopes. Facts and figures.

A complete list of my checking targets over the many years I spent in Doubt could fill this chapter. And that's no exaggeration — though I must confess I'm thinking I should probably calculate the number of words I'd need for my list, along with the space available in an average chapter, and then check and recheck that math a few times, just to be sure. (A little OCD humor.)

Checking has been a constant feature of my life with OCD. It has also proved to be the most alluring trapdoor when I'm stuck in Doubt. Time and again in my worst years, my doubt bully would pose an anxiety-provoking "what if" question, and I, almost without thinking, would attempt to prevent the potential catastrophic consequences by physically checking to make sure that they either hadn't happened in the past or couldn't happen in the future.

In each case, the checking accomplished all of the following:

1. Relieved some of my anxiety — temporarily.
2. Reinforced the brief, but real, payoff of my compulsive actions.

3. Led to more "what if" questions that, in turn, led to more checking.
4. Again relieved some of my anxiety — temporarily.
5. Again reinforced the brief, but real, payoff of my compulsive actions.
6. Again led to more "what if" questions that, in turn, led to more checking.

For OCD checkers such as myself, the act of checking is akin to treasure hunting in a dark cave and discovering a hatch marked "Gold." We pry it up, look inside, and fall in, only to find ourselves even deeper in the cave. We get back on our feet, start looking around, and come across another hatch marked "Diamonds." We pry it open, look inside, and again fall deeper into the cave. This is how trapdoors work, and this is how checking leaves us ever more stuck in Doubt.

At the beginning of this book, I mentioned how common I've found garage-door checking to be. It seems to be human nature to question our actions from time to time, acting *with* doubt in a healthy, constructive way. That said, I've also found that a good many of my non-OCD friends and acquaintances have, through their own fear-based doubts, fallen through the same checking trapdoors that I have. Although they tend to find their way back out far more quickly and easily than those of us with OCD, they too waste a great deal of time and energy in counterproductive checking drills.

Take Andy Ellis, a fifty-nine-year-old radio engineer with whom I work at CBS/San Francisco. The two of us go back many, many years, and he has always struck me as one of the most grounded, rational, and analytical people I've ever met. Andy approaches his life much as he approaches his engineering work around the station — in a methodical, reasoned, and deliberate way.

In August 2008, Andy was diagnosed with prostate cancer, a blow that hit all of us who work with him, despite Andy's own assurances that, because of his doctor's early detection, his prognosis was excellent. About a month later, Andy told me that he was keeping a journal of his new life as a cancer patient and, knowing my fascination with memoir, asked if I'd be interested in looking at what he'd written.

I, of course, jumped at the opportunity and was drawn in immediately by Andy's candor, his engineering analysis (complete with diagrams and precise technical data), and his disarming sense of humor. In typical Andy fashion, he opens his journal with a joke that goes something like this: A condemned engineer is lying on his back, about to lose his head to a guillotine blade. Something happens, though, and the guillotine jams. The engineer gets up, looks over the mechanism, and tells the executioner, "Well, *here's* where your problem is!"

Andy's intent was to point out just how programmed an engineer's brain is to solve problems, and his journal certainly makes that case, fact by fact, observation by observation. The more I read, the more fascinated I became by Andy's ability to face a frightening life challenge with such little outward fear. One day I told him about this project and asked if he would be open to helping me understand his strategies for handling all the new uncertainty in his life.

What I've learned from Andy in our subsequent conversations has corroborated, perhaps more than anything else in my research, the parallels between OCD and fear-based doubt, even for the most rational people out there. Andy, I learned — despite his engineer's logic — finds himself falling through the very same checking trapdoor that has enticed and ensnared me for much of my adult life.

For Andy, the checking trapdoor is marked "Answers." He knows he's working with some of the best-qualified doctors around and is getting some of the finest cancer treatment available. He knows (at least intellectually) that — much as we nontechnical sorts at the station must trust him and his colleagues to keep us on the air — he must trust his doctors to do their best to keep him alive. He knows his inner engineer (with its hallmark intellect-based doubt) has served him well, helping him formulate intelligent, important questions to ask his doctors. But still he finds himself falling victim to his own fear-based doubt and the "what if" question his bully poses again and again: *What if your doctors are missing something?*

Andy confides in me that he has taken to scouring the Internet for hours on end, researching articles, looking for facts and figures or treatment strategies that his doctors might have overlooked. When he occasionally finds an item that hints at the existence of some little-known information, his find only draws him deeper into his research.

"It's wasted time," he tells me, explaining that he fully understands that his time spent researching could instead be spent with his family or used to tackle any of a variety of far more productive projects. So why does Andy get caught up in his online checking?

For the very same reason, I would say, that I spent years scouring my car, bumper to bumper, after driving trips to confirm the lack of blood or other evidence that I had run over someone. Both Andy and I fell into the trap of trying to rid ourselves of our fear-based doubts by looking for answers. Yes, Andy's Googling seems reasonable, given his circumstances. But I think he'd agree that, in reality, it's every bit as futile as my car inspections.

TRAPDOOR 2: REASSURANCE-SEEKING

The next two trapdoors I want to examine look a whole lot like those associated with physical checking, but they're just different enough that it makes sense to explore them separately.

The first of these, reassurance-seeking, is a familiar one for Jared Kant, a twenty-five-year-old medical researcher I've gotten to know through our shared involvement with the national OC Foundation. As Jared details in his inspiring memoir, *The Thought That Counts*, he was diagnosed with OCD at the age of eleven and spent years battling the extremes of the disorder, at one point being hospitalized because of the severity of his obsessions and compulsions.

Like me, Jared has long been plagued by obsessive "what if" questions about his abilities and judgment. And, like me, he wound up developing a laundry list of checking drills to try to counter the distress of his obsessions. As we both discovered, however, our physical checking was never enough, especially since we couldn't trust our judgment. *What if you didn't check correctly, or sufficiently?* our bullies would ask. And that's where reassurance-seeking would kick in for us.

Jared offers up this example: He is just out of college and renting a new apartment. To celebrate his new freedom, he lights a stick of incense — something he couldn't do in college or while living with his parents. Taking precautions that his local fire chief would have hailed with a proclamation, Jared puts the stick on a metal dish, and the dish on a nonflammable holder. He positions a shot glass to catch the ashes.

Ah, freedom. This is the life.

But the next morning when Jared awakens, he begins to panic, wondering how he can possibly ensure that his apartment is fire safe before he leaves for the day. His bully is at the ready with a series of button-pushing questions: *What if the ashes are still smoldering? What if the stick itself is still hot?*

Jared flushes the ashes, along with a gallon of water, down the sink. He carefully disposes of the sticks. He thinks he can leave now.

But what if you missed something, some sign of the still-existing hazard?

At this point, Jared starts checking the floor, looking for burn marks or other signs that the apartment might at some point have caught fire. He sees nothing. *But what if you're not looking carefully enough?* his bully taunts. Again and again, Jared inspects the floor. At long last he breaks free of his checking and heads for the door, only to be drawn back for one "final" look.

Jared is trapped (thanks to his "checking" trapdoor), and he knows it. He's also certain he can't leave his apartment and handle the distress of obsessing about it all day. So, before he can help himself, he heads for another trapdoor — this one marked "Second Opinion." He phones his father and explains his concerns.

"So, in your opinion," Jared asks his dad, "what's the likelihood of anything going wrong while I'm out?"

Compulsive reassurance-seeking is a trapdoor because, like all compulsions, it only leaves the seeker deeper in Doubt. Sure, there's a temporary payoff. Jared inevitably felt relieved after his father told him, in so many words, that there wasn't a chance in hell that his apartment was going to burn down. But I'm also willing to bet that within minutes of hanging up the phone, Jared was questioning whether he'd adequately described the potential dangers to his father and was tempted to call back. Either way, Jared had reinforced this obsessive-compulsive cycle, meaning that the next time his physical checking failed him, he was that much more likely to seek reassurance.

Reassurance-seeking presents a huge challenge to friends and relatives of those of us with OCD. It's only natural that they would want to do all they can to comfort us — especially when we come to them in agony, all but begging for comfort. They want to help, and so they give us what we're looking for. Unfortunately, though, they then become part of the problem, "enabling" us (to borrow a term from the twelve-step world) and further reinforcing our distress-relief cycles. Because of the confusion this reassurance-seeking creates, OCD therapists often bring spouses and parents into the treatment process, at least enough to help them understand why their best-intentioned efforts to help their loved ones may only compound the problem.

This strategy proved to be key in my own recovery, as I had become addicted to Samantha's reassurances. Day after day I would call Sam from work, pleading for her opinion on one thing or another.

I justified the constant disruptions by assuring her that I'd never be able to get through my day without hearing from her that I had handled the current source of my anxiety correctly. Ultimately, my therapist helped wean me off this compulsion by restricting my reassurance questions to those I could fit on an index card and limiting the time I could seek reassurance to one fifteen-minute sit-down session with Sam every night. One of the proudest moments of my recovery was the night I sat down with Samantha for our daily "card time," as we came to call it, prepared to jam in as many items as possible, but surprised both of us by taking out the 3 x 5 card and ripping it in half.

While reassurance-seeking is a pretty obvious compulsion for those of us with OCD, the trapdoor it presents for those simply stuck in Doubt is a bit more camouflaged. It's natural for us to seek the opinions of our colleagues and loved ones; and when our intellect-based doubts are driving this checking, it's healthy. Asking your best friend what she thinks about your desire to change jobs makes all the sense in the world: she knows you well, and her feedback can help you make a good decision. But what if it's fear, not caution or curiosity, driving your "opinion seeking" — which, in reality, is a search for reassurance, not opinions?

Allow me to introduce you to another of our tour guides, Terry, a psychology professor I met through my OCD outreach. Terry chairs the psychology department at her college and knows a great deal about cognitive distortions from both her professional training and her teaching. But she also knows firsthand how these distortions can twist our thinking. Terry spent much of her life battling depression; at her worst, she tells me, she could have been a poster child for cognitive distortions. Today, Terry works hard to keep her depression in check, but in so doing, she occasionally finds herself falling through the trapdoors that her fear-based doubt has set, and reassurance-seeking is certainly one of them.

She offers this example: One afternoon while she's grading papers in her office, a colleague shows up and asks to talk. He tells her he was insulted by a comment she'd made in a recent conversation. Terry is taken aback by this news, and after her colleague leaves, she quickly slips into fear-based doubt. First come the black-and-white assumptions: *If one person thinks I'm thoughtless, then I must be.* And *If this colleague thinks I'm thoughtless, then everyone else must too.* And *Certainly* no one else *would have been so thoughtless.* Next comes the catastrophizing: *What if this colleague never forgives me because what I said was so terrible?* And *What if this act of thoughtlessness ruins the trust I've built up with my other colleagues, once they find out?*

As Terry's fear-based doubt grows, so too does her distress. She has a busy day ahead of her and can't afford to get wrapped up in this uncertainty, so she decides to take action. She heads to another colleague's office and shares the whole story — her original conversation, the male colleague's concern, her reaction. She asks this second colleague for her opinion about the whole matter. Had she been out of line?

Terry gets the reassurance she is looking for: her friend assures her she is not a thoughtless person. Terry feels better. She leaves her friend's office ready to get back to work. But within minutes she's wondering if she should get at least one more opinion — just to make sure her friend's assessment was accurate, and just to make sure she can get on with her day.

Did Terry do any harm in seeking out her friend's reassurance? No. And in the end, she was able to resist the urge to seek the reassurance of additional friends, so her stay in Doubt proved relatively brief. But Terry knows this outcome could have gone the other way, as it has for her in the past. It would have been easy to get sucked into spending her entire afternoon looking for reassurance that she wasn't a bad person. She knows this is how such trapdoors work.

TRAPDOOR 3: RUMINATING

For all the time I have wasted on checking and reassurance-seeking, those two trapdoors have proved far less menacing in my own life than the one marked "Ruminating." I've spent so much time doing this "mental checking," as it's known, that I could fill an entire book with examples. (Oh yeah, I already have.)

As I explain in *Rewind, Replay, Repeat*, I have developed an uncanny ability to rewind and replay "virtual videos" of even the most mundane incidents in my life: work conversations, lane changes in my car, trips through a grocery store, you name it. I can back up these "tapes" (as I call them) and replay them again and again, even pausing to freeze a frame, much as I can with my real-life TiVo. And this is precisely what I would do when I was looking for answers, typically once I'd exhausted my checking and reassurance-seeking options.

Let's say I'd heard a baby cry as I was walking through a busy shopping mall. Immediately my bully would start with the "what-if" questions: *What if you unknowingly smacked into that woman carrying an infant as she was walking by? What if that baby grows up with brain damage?* Yadda, yadda.

Before I knew it, I would find myself heading back through the mall, retracing my route and looking for the woman or any signs of a medical emergency. Finding nothing, I would call Samantha from my cell phone and plead for her assurances: "Do you think I would have known if I'd elbowed some kid?" "Surely the mother would have hollered at me if she thought I was responsible, right?"

When I ran out of checking and reassurance-seeking options, I would start my exhaustive process of mentally checking the entire trigger. With skills honed through years of practice, I would piece together the sequence of events immediately before, during, and after the moment I'd heard the cry. I would conjure up vivid images of myself and the crowd and the woman with the baby, and I would reconstruct the soundtrack of piped-in Muzak, leaky iPods, random conversations in multiple languages, and the squeaks of nearby strollers and shoes.

Putting everything in motion next, I would try to figure out just how close I'd come to the infant and assess the probabilities of my having made contact. The catch, as always, was that the key scene in my tape — in this case, the moment I passed the woman and baby — was just enough out of focus to hide the details I was craving. And so I would replay the sequence again, and again, and again.

Ruminating is often confused with obsessing, typically among newly diagnosed sufferers but occasionally among inexperienced treatment providers as well. This mental checking is done strictly in one's head, much like obsessing. But, unlike obsessing, it is willful and deliberate. Ruminating is, in fact, a compulsive activity engaged in for the sole purpose of relieving distress. In the above example, I am obsessing about having harmed some poor infant; in reaction to this obsessing, I am compulsively re-creating the incident in my head. I may not feel as if I'm in control of this compulsion, but I am. Willfully and deliberately, I am choosing to reconstruct and replay the trigger again and again — a decision no different, really, from my choosing to walk back through the mall or pick up the phone to call Sam. This distinction between compulsion and obsession may be a subtle one, but, as we will see in later chapters, it's important.

Before I went public with my story, I often wondered what things look like inside "normal" heads. Are most people equipped with the same virtual home-theater system that I have? If so, do they too employ theirs to review events and conversations over and over again?

The answers, I've found, are Yes and Yes. Perhaps because of the title of my first book, I tend to hear from a lot of people about the virtual video-watching — or ruminating — that they do. Most people probably don't spend a fraction of the time on it that I did, and I suspect they're not nearly as adept at it as I am (not to brag about my expert OCD skills or anything). But they do know this trapdoor and often know it all too well.

My friend Lisa reminded me of this over coffee recently. As I explained the focus of my new book, I noticed Lisa nodding her head. I asked if she could relate to the trapdoors I was describing, and without missing a beat she offered up an example that I imagine many people can relate to well.

Lisa had been out on a first date a couple of days earlier with a guy she wanted to see again. The two of them had really hit it off, she told me, and they talked about reconnecting soon, but he hadn't called. Leaning across the table toward me, Lisa confided that she'd been calling her answering machine from work to see if perhaps he'd left a message.

"Okay, there's the checking trapdoor," I offered far too quickly, probably sounding like some wannabe shrink. "What was going through your mind during these couple of days?"

In so many words, Lisa explained that her fear-based doubt bully was posing all kinds of nagging "what if" questions, including whether she'd said or done anything offensive during the date.

"And how did you deal with that?" I asked.

"Well, I wasted a bunch of time replaying the whole date in my head," Lisa explained.

"Ah. The 'ruminating' trapdoor!" Dr. Bell was on a roll.

You'll be glad to know that I didn't charge Lisa for our "session," though I didn't hear from her for several weeks, despite our plans to talk again soon. Hmmm. Perhaps she was offended by all my questioning. What exactly did I ask? Better rewind the tape and replay the conversation . . .

TRAPDOOR 4: PROTECTING

The first three trapdoors we've explored all offer the same false lure: verification. "Check here," they taunt, "and you can be sure that everything is or will be okay."

The next trapdoor works a bit differently. Instead of offering veri-fication, it offers protection. In the OCD world, these traps include excessive washing and cleaning, repeating, counting, hoarding, and compulsive praying. On the surface, these are very different behaviors, but each one is a ritual aimed at warding off some feared consequence.

Take the compulsion known as repeating, a familiar one to my good friend Carole Johnson. If you've read my first book, you've already met Carole, and you know the critical role she has played in my life. It was she who inspired me to go public with my story, and it was from her that I learned so much about the process of *making belief*. Carole is a remarkable woman in many ways, but my main rea-son for asking her to serve as a tour guide here is this rather dubious distinction: Carole has spent more time in the Shadow of Doubt than anyone else I have ever met.

Carole is seventy-nine years old. As she recounts in her auto-biography, *The Heart Has Its Own Memory*, she has battled OCD her entire life, but went undiagnosed until 1985. That means she spent some fifty-five years not knowing there was a biological explanation for the thoughts and compulsions that plagued her. In the absence of that knowledge, Carole let her mind come up with a variety of theo-ries, including the especially disturbing notion that she was possessed by the devil. For much of her life, she simply accepted that her chal-lenges were a punishment from which she could not escape. It pains me to think about the distress she endured.

During Carole's many years in Doubt, she developed a series of so-called repeating compulsions — rituals she performed in hopes of protecting herself and others from harm. For whatever strange reasons, three became Carole's magic number — and, by extension, her most troublesome trapdoor. When she was looking to "clear" bad thoughts, she found herself compelled to repeat sequences in sets of three. These sequences ranged from chewing food three times to flipping light switches on and off precisely three, six, or nine times in a row — all in order to ward off catastrophic consequences.

Carole's "what if" questions (i.e., obsessions) usually end with some scenario in which harm befalls someone she loves because she has failed to protect them. Her compulsive urges tend to involve repeating rituals that are entirely unrelated to the nature of her fears; in this sense, they are the result of what some psychologists term "magical thinking."

Let's say Carole walks into a grocery store on a bad OCD day and happens to notice some small item on the floor — a box of teabags, for example. She picks it up and puts it back on the shelf, but as she does her doubt bully poses these questions in rapid succession: *What if you don't replace the item "correctly"? What if your failure to replace the box correctly leads to something bad happening to someone* (let's say Carole's daughter, Frankie)? And *What if Frankie is in a car crash because you failed to protect her?*

Carole attempts to ignore her bully. She knows its taunting is ridiculous. But by the time she reaches the bread aisle her mind has filled with graphic images of Frankie's car in a ditch, her mangled body nearby. The image is unbearable, and with every passing second Carole's anxiety grows.

Clear the thought, her bully suggests. This is only possible, Carole knows from so many similar OCD cycles, by indulging her compulsive urge to repeat the replacing motion exactly three times.

There you go, the bully taunts. *Make the box "just right" on the shelf.*

Carole fights the urge and goes on with her shopping, but the images of Frankie grow increasingly vivid, and her anxiety just keeps building. She wonders how she'll get through the day when she's this distracted. Before she knows it, she is back in the tea aisle.

She removes the box and replaces it three times. But her bully suggests that perhaps one cycle of three might not do the trick, so she repeats the sequence another three times.

No. Still not there.

One more time, Carole decides. She goes through the motion a seventh, eighth, and ninth time, and finally finds the relief she was seeking. In a heartbeat, the weight of the world is off of her shoulders. Frankie is safe.

Greatly relieved, Carole walks toward the checkout stand with her other groceries, only to pass a stray bottle of vitamins on the floor in another section ...

Carole's repeating patterns may be hard for most people to relate to. I myself have never felt compelled to do anything in sets of three (or any other number), and I remember being thoroughly confused by my earliest conversations with Carole about our respective compulsions. It took years for me to figure out that we were both, in our own ways, falling through trapdoors marked "Protection."

On those countless occasions when I found myself stuck at a sink, scrubbing my hands in scalding hot water, just in case I might be carrying some horrific virus I could pass along to others, I too was trying to protect those I might otherwise harm. Likewise, washers who obsess about catching deadly germs from other people scrub away to protect themselves.

So what does this trapdoor look like for those who don't suffer from OCD? From the examples I've collected, I want to share with you one that gets to the very heart of the uncertainty distress that drives us when we're stuck in Doubt.

Sarah Allen Benton is a thirty-two-year-old licensed mental health counselor at a college in Boston. She is also a recovering alcoholic. As she recounts with great candor in her courageous new book, *Understanding the High-Functioning Alcoholic*, Sarah began binge drinking at the age of fourteen. She experienced blackouts and other dangerous consequences from her drinking throughout her high school, college, and young adult years before finding her way into a twelve-step program at the age of twenty-seven.

Sarah's journal entries, which she shares in her book, illustrate the tragically enormous toll that excessive drinking can take on one's life. They also offer those of us outside the world of addiction a rare glimpse at the challenges an alcoholic faces in deciding to become sober.

For Sarah, these challenges extended far beyond getting and staying sober. They included a whole new set of fear-based doubts surrounding her identity and the way that her friends would see her. She had built an entire life around her drinking, one in which she was a social, fun, and exciting person that people wanted to be around.

What if your friends won't want to be with the new, sober you? Sarah's doubt bully would ask. *What if you won't be able to fit in? What if you wind up isolated because you can't drink anymore?*

The "what if" questions that plagued Sarah in her early recovery days strike me as remarkably similar to the fear-based doubts that we with OCD face: catastrophic in nature (posing the threat of lifelong isolation) and founded in black-and-white assumptions (either all her friends will like the new Sarah, or they'll all hate her). And while Sarah did not develop the need to flip light switches on and off three times, or scrub her hands, or perform any other compulsive rituals, I believe she did find herself heading again and again to this trapdoor marked "Protection."

As Sarah explained to me, after several months of being sober she continued putting herself in places she knew she shouldn't be — namely, bars and social events involving alcohol — not because she wanted to be there (it was torture, she said) but because she wanted to protect her friendships. Intellectually, she understood that, as a newly sober alcoholic, she should avoid situations centered on drinking; but because of her bully's taunting, she felt compelled to put herself in these situations for protection. I would argue that this sort of protecting is very much a trap: the more importance she placed on being with her friends in drinking situations, the more she used this twisted approach — and not authenticity — to keep her friendships alive: "I went to bar A with friends. Now, won't they expect me at bar B? I'd better go there as well."

TRAPDOOR 5: FIXING

Of the six trapdoors that can keep us stuck in Doubt, the one marked "Fixing" stands alone. Unlike the other five, this one has far less to do with feared consequences than it does with the (false) relief it offers from what we might call unassigned distress. Sometimes things just don't "feel" right, and we look for ways to fix this distressing feeling. In the OCD world this translates to compulsions involving order and symmetry.

My friend Matt is a forty-year-old lawyer. We met many years ago while working at a radio station in Northern California. This was in the days before I went public with my OCD, but we learned through a mutual friend that we shared a common "challenge," which we soon discovered was OCD.

Matt is one of the sharpest guys I've ever met, so I remember being surprised when he first confided in me how anxious he was about taking his law school entrance exams.

"You know this stuff inside and out," I told him.

"Yeah," he said, just before scanning the room for anyone who might be in earshot. "But what if I can't get the papers on my desk lined up just right during the test?" As he explained to me, his bully likes to play a game with him, convincing him that he can't possibly concentrate or get anything done (including a test) until nearby items are positioned correctly.

Fortunately, he aced both the LSAT and the bar exam on his first try — but only, he tells me, because he knew the material so well that he could work around the time constraints of feeding his bully.

For Matt and others with similar compulsions, symmetry and order can pose serious life challenges that require the attention of professional ERP therapists. But, as I've come to find, "fixing" is hardly the exclusive domain of those with OCD. To help make this point, I turn to the most carefree, grounded, and well-adjusted person I know: my wife.

Samantha surprised the heck out of me some months ago, as we were discussing my list of trapdoors and her uncanny ability to steer clear of them. "Oh, I do that one," she said, referring to fixing.

"What?!" I couldn't believe it. "No, you don't."

"Yes, I do," Sam insisted. "I need symmetry when it comes to sensation."

Sam went on to explain that should she happen to bite the inside of her mouth on the right side, she needs to deliberately bite the left side as well. Likewise, should she happen to scratch her left palm, she feels compelled to scratch the right one.

"Why?" I ask.

"Just to make it feel right. Just to fix things."

And all this time I thought *I* was the quirky one!

This is probably a good place for me to say a few words about OCPD, or obsessive compulsive personality disorder, as it's known. This psychological challenge is very different from OCD and often creates a lot of confusion in discussions about compulsive ordering or neatness.

People with OCPD tend to like order. They are often what we might think of as "neat freaks," and their homes, cars, and offices are typically immaculate. For those of you old enough to remember the TV show *The Odd Couple*, think of Felix Unger.

A key distinction between OCPD and OCD is that people with OCPD draw pleasure from their compulsive ordering or cleaning activities. Those of us with OCD most definitely do not. This topic comes up often in my outreach talks. Almost without exception when I ask for questions, someone will raise his hand and tell me how he tends to arrange his socks in a certain order or stack his soup cans in perfect columns. "Is this OCD?" he'll ask. My answer usually involves three questions:

- Do you dislike doing this activity?
- Does this activity get in the way of your day?
- Do you become anxious if you can't do this activity?

After carefully qualifying that I'm not a doctor (one of my own compulsive disclosure rituals), I explain to the socks-and-soup guy that if he answered no to these questions, he's probably not battling OCD. I also offer up this example from my own life: I have one of the neatest walk-in closets in America. Well, actually, that's only half true. Samantha is, shall we say, *not* a neat freak (she has no OCD ordering issues, I assure you, despite her sensation-symmetry quirk): her half of the closet looks like unsorted laundry flung randomly over hangers. *My* half is nothing short of a work of art. Starting from the left and working toward the right, my suits and sport coats, dress pants, casual pants, long-sleeved dress shirts, short-sleeved dress shirts, long-sleeved casual shirts, short-sleeved casual shirts, and, finally, T-shirts are arrayed in perfect order. And, yes, the hangers are color coded.

But that's just my OCD, right?

Wrong. Here's why:

I love my half of the closet. I actually get a kick out of arranging the clothes items. (It brings me pleasure.) I can't imagine being late for work because I'm stuck rearranging the hangers. (My "ordering" does not get in the way of my day.) And, while I enjoy seeing my clothes hanging as if in some department store, I can't ever recall feeling uneasy when they're not. In fact, recently, I've been so absorbed writing this book that my half of the closet doesn't look that different from Samantha's. (I may take some serious ribbing from Sam about this, but the state of the closet itself does not make me anxious.)

Contrast all this with my penchant for picking up rocks and twigs — a "protecting" compulsion during my worst years aimed at

addressing the uncertainty posed by my doubt bully's nagging question *What if one of those things kicks up into the spokes of a bicycle wheel
and someone gets hurt?* I *hated* having to pick up sidewalk debris, often
watched by nearby pedestrians wondering what the heck I was doing.
(I definitely derived no pleasure from this activity.) You can imagine
how time-consuming this process could be. (It definitely got in the
way of my day.) And during my recovery years, when I tried to resist
picking up the rocks and twigs I passed, I often found myself forced
to double back several blocks later because of my seeming inability to
deal with the doubt discomfort. (Refraining from this compulsion
made me very anxious indeed.)

While OCD and OCPD may look a lot alike, and while many of
us with OCD may also have OCPD tendencies, these two diagnoses
are very different, and the distinctions between them are important.
Most relevant here is that OCD is the result of fear-based doubt;
OCPD is not.

TRAPDOOR 6: AVOIDING

And now to the final stop on our trapdoor tour.

The sign on this one reads "Avoiding," and just below it are the
words "Welcome One and All." Its lure is that universal. OCD sufferers, non-OCD checkers, reassurance-seekers, ruminators, protec-
tors, and fixers — all are drawn to this door.

In the OCD world, avoidance is what you might call the ultimate
compulsion. It refers to the practice of deliberately avoiding those
events and situations that trigger our anxiety. By avoiding those triggers, the thinking goes, we can avoid the compulsions they ultimately
spawn.

But isn't avoiding compulsions what we're after?

Yes. But not at the expense of living our lives! And if avoidance
becomes our answer to the distress of fear-based doubt, then we're

feeding the OCD cycle in the very same fashion as if we were performing a ritual such as washing or checking.

Put another way: if my bully, Octi, starts taunting me with "what if" questions about an activity, and I respond to them by simply avoiding that activity, then I have fed Octi a doubt-nut and, in so doing, I have made him stronger and hungrier.

Amy can help us understand this point. She is a popular, driven, and very happy high school student. A cheerleader with an infectious smile and poise beyond her years, she exudes confidence, and I can't imagine anyone would ever know the extent to which doubt has at times consumed her life. Her commitment to doing exposure therapy has helped Amy immensely, and her recovery is a true OCD success story. During her many years in Doubt, though, Amy battled a fairly common OCD fear of acting on aggressive thoughts that she herself has always found repulsive and ridiculous.

"Take knives," she tells me, explaining her longtime fear of being with someone else in a kitchen, with so many knives within reach. "What if somehow something overtook me and I stabbed that person?"

Amy insists she has never really believed she'd stab anyone in her kitchen (or elsewhere), but the uncertainty was so distressing at times that she often found it easier just to avoid the kitchen (or other places with knives) altogether. By doing so, of course, Amy was falling through the trapdoor of avoidance.

Today Amy understands how debilitating the simple act of avoidance can be. But she, like I and so many others battling OCD, had to learn this the hard way, giving up one aspect of her life after another simply to avoid her triggers. If staying clear of kitchens was helpful, staying clear of houses with knives inside was even better. And what about stores that sell knives? Wouldn't it make sense to keep out of them as well?

I'm guessing that you too have fallen through a few avoidance trapdoors in your life, though it's quite possible that you didn't even realize it at the time. I had to laugh when I asked my sister, Mandi, to be our tour guide for this particular false exit. Mandi, bless her heart, is a classic worrier and would be the first to admit that, while not clinically obsessive compulsive like her brother, she has spent far more time than most of her friends and colleagues stuck in Doubt and falling through trapdoors.

"I can't really think of any avoidance examples," she apologized, when I called to make my request.

"Hmmmm," I deadpanned. "Do me a favor and give it some thought."

Sure enough, my phone rang the next morning, and it was Mandi, laughing at the other end. "So, I have an example . . . well, actually, quite a long list of examples for you."

I can't honestly remember all the items on Mandi's list, but here are a few:

- No watching medical TV shows, in order to avoid dealing with those nagging questions of *What if you or the kids came down with that condition?*
- No turning left without a signal onto a busy street or highway because she tends to be overcautious and worries that the driver behind her might get angry.
- And no being the last one to leave the school where she teaches, so she can avoid being the one responsible for setting the alarm system, which she might do incorrectly.

The inconveniences that Mandi's avoidance creates pale in comparison to the many serious problems Amy faced in rearranging her entire life to avoid being around knives during her worst OCD years. But, as we've seen, all the false exits that promise to lead us out of the Shadow of Doubt — whether we are battling OCD or just everyday fear-based doubts — only lead us further into the dark.

Because these parallels exist, I want next to introduce you to the combination of strategies, gleaned from both the OCD and non-OCD worlds, that have shown me the only way out of Doubt — strategies that, together, comprise the ten steps necessary to *make belief*.

KEY POINTS

- When stuck "in Doubt" and searching for a way out, we often fall through one or more of the following six "trap-doors":

  1. **Checking:** physically searching for verification that some feared consequence did not, or will not, happen.
  2. **Reassurance-seeking:** asking for the assurances of others that some feared consequence did not, or will not, happen.
  3. **Ruminating:** mentally replaying events, conversations, and other sequences in search of verification that some feared consequence did not, or will not, happen.
  4. **Protecting:** performing rituals (such as repeating patterns) and acting in unproductive ways for the sole purpose of warding off feared consequences.
  5. **Fixing:** performing rituals (often relating to symmetry) for the sole purpose of making things "feel" right.
  6. **Avoiding:** deliberately avoiding events that trigger anxiety; this can be thought of as the ultimate compulsion.

- OCPD (obsessive compulsive personality disorder) is a personality disorder often confused with OCD but very different, in that it involves neither obsessions nor compulsions. It is often marked by an excessive drive for perfection, neatness, or order.

PART TWO

MAKING BELIEF

(TEN STEPS OUT WHEN STUCK IN DOUBT)

CHAPTER FOUR

Reverence

First Principle of Making Belief

I n August 1997, I was thirty-three, happily married with two precious daughters, and holding one of the most coveted radio jobs in California.

I was also living a lie. And miserable. The guy my listeners drove home with every afternoon — and, for that matter, the guy most everyone in my off-air world knew me as — might have seemed pretty together. But the guy they didn't know was anything but.

This guy was stuck — make that entrenched — in Doubt, stumbling his way through one trapdoor after another, lost, confused, deflated, and bitter.

I had, at this juncture, been through five therapists, two kinds of medications, several ministers, countless books, and every other resource I could think of, searching in vain for a way out of the doubt. I was doing everything I could to get better, I told myself, and yet I was still spending hours each day checking and ruminating and confessing and seeking reassurance. I was at my wits' end and ready to quit.

It was in this frame of mind that I wound up in my backyard hammock one hot, sticky night. And it was with this desperation that I found myself offering up a bargain with the universe that would forever change my world.

"Show me how to turn around this crazy life," I mumbled to the vast blanket of stars overhead, "and I'll share my story with anyone who will listen." The words just kind of came out, and more as a taunting challenge than anything else — something akin, really, to what a parent might say to a child: Keep your room immaculate all year, and I'll buy you a pony. Still, I waited a few days, just to see what would happen. Nothing. No instruction book came floating down from the heavens.

In the weeks that followed, though, something profound did happen: I somehow turned that bargain on its head. I told myself I was going to share my story — an inspiring tale of recovering from the worst of OCD — understanding at some core level that doing so would, in fact, turn my life around. I knew that, as a longtime public speaker with at least some name recognition, I was in a great position to go public with my success story. Only one minor problem: I had no success story to share.

And that's when I first stumbled onto the concept of Greater Good and the very key to making belief. Without calling it out as such, I wound up identifying a Greater Good goal for myself. This goal was much bigger than my OCD and driven by two distinct objectives: first, to enhance my own sense of purpose by giving meaning to all I'd been through with my OCD battles; and second, to be of service to others by offering a first-person account of living with, and recovering from, the very worst of this disorder.

Although I couldn't have known it that night in 1997, these two concepts of *purpose* and *service* would prove to be the most powerful motivators I've ever known, the driving force behind my OCD recovery and outreach, and the essence of everything else that I hope to share in this book.

All that I did know in the wake of my commitment to share my OCD success story was that I'd better figure out a way to start finding some success! I needed a plan. Fortunately, that same inner Felix Unger who enjoys color coding the hangers in my closet was able to kick into action, and before I knew it I had devised a scheme to jumpstart my recovery.

I resolved that beginning on my thirty-fourth birthday — which was just weeks away — and for precisely one year, I would keep a detailed journal of my life with OCD. Better yet, I would write everything down on 3 x 5 cards, so I could neatly categorize my observations, like the shirts and pants in my closet: one stack for obsessions, another for compulsions, a third for triumphs, a fourth for setbacks, and so on. I would reconnect with my behavior therapist, whom I had dismissed after she failed to fix me (note my mind-set then!), with a new commitment to give my all to ERP therapy. And I would try to teach myself everything there is to know about the mechanics of belief.

This final commitment struck me, even then, as the most important of all. If my problems stemmed from being stuck in Doubt, then my salvation lay in understanding the antidote to doubt: belief.

What I needed was a road map, an instruction manual, a blueprint, if you will, for making belief.

A BLUEPRINT FOR BELIEVING

So how does one draw up building plans for something as abstract as belief? And just what was it, anyway, that I was looking to believe in? I hadn't a clue how to answer these questions when I first started plotting my quest, but my approach to finding out went something like this:

First, I asked myself, "What is it that I doubt?" The short answer was "Everything!" But when I forced myself to be more specific, I realized that my doubts — at least as my bully presented them to me — fell into three specific areas: doubts about myself (my abilities, judgment, and motives); doubts about others (their abilities, judgment, and motives); and doubts about life itself (its meaning, value, opportunities, and the like).

These, I decided, must also be the targets of my belief. What I needed were guidelines for believing in myself, in others, and in life. Drawing on a "mission statement" I'd written years ago as part of a goal-setting exercise, I next listed the qualities that I felt characterized those people I knew who had the ability to *make belief*:

- People who believe in themselves demonstrate integrity, strength, initiative, and release (letting go of what they cannot control).
- People who believe in others demonstrate respect, compassion, generosity, and trust.
- People who believe in life demonstrate passion, perspective, involvement, and faith.

I launched my journaling year with a commitment to study these twelve qualities and think about how I might use them to help me stand up to my bully. I had every intention of working with the principles behind them. I never expected, though, that they would present themselves to me in one unified model.

It happened on Day 2 of my Crash Course in Believing, as I came to call this year of journaling. I was sitting in my parked car, mulling over the twelve words I'd chosen to study. In one of those weird Aha! moments that you can never really explain — and that typically make you sound pretty dang silly when you try — I suddenly found myself grabbing for one of my handy index cards and scribbling on it the top and side views of a pyramid into which I began inserting my dozen "belief" words. Very soon I had a rough sketch of the three-sided, four-level pyramid that you see in figure 4.1.

I still marvel at the way my blueprint came together, and as I type these words, nearly twelve years later, I'm looking across my desk at the three-inch cardboard model I built from it that same day when I got home from work. (I contemplated including a pop-up version in this book, but found myself wondering whether someone might poke an eye out on its pointy apex; guess I'm not entirely over the whole harm hang-up yet.)

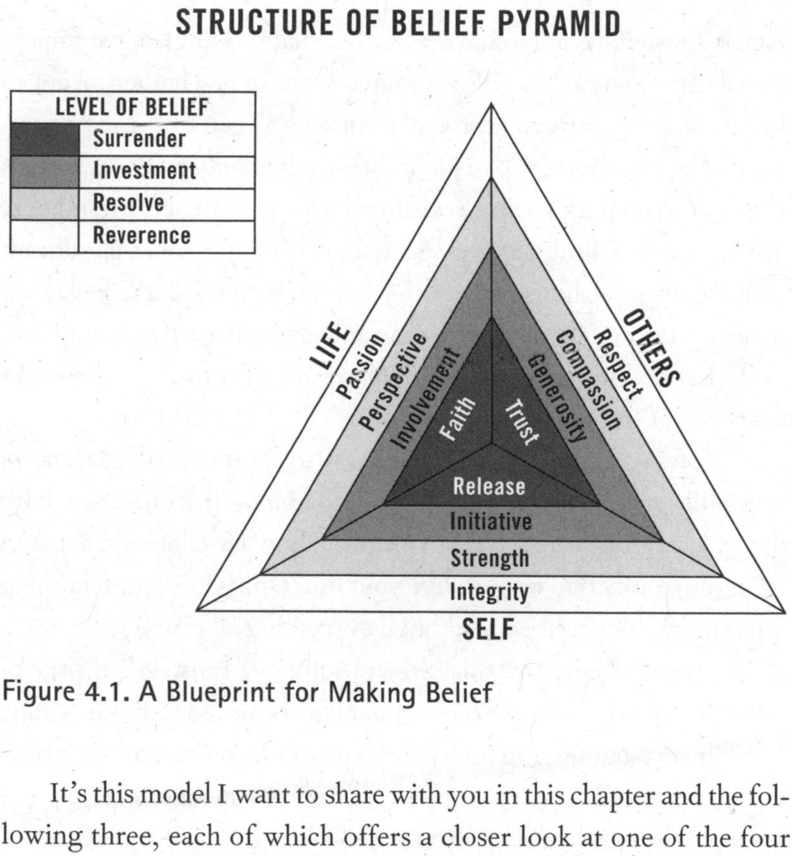

STRUCTURE OF BELIEF PYRAMID

Figure 4.1. A Blueprint for Making Belief

It's this model I want to share with you in this chapter and the following three, each of which offers a closer look at one of the four levels of my "structure of belief" pyramid — reverence, resolve, investment, and surrender. I've opted to focus on these four tiers of the model, and not the twelve words they comprise, largely because the latter are simply my own vocabulary words for describing specific aspects of these fundamental principles of believing — in myself, in others, and in life. You might very well use twelve different words. What's universal, I believe, are the principles themselves and the specific strategies that grew out of them, strategies that I've come to see as *the ten steps out when stuck in Doubt.*

STEP 1: CHOOSE TO SEE THE UNIVERSE AS FRIENDLY

Albert Einstein is said to have remarked that the single most important decision any of us will ever have to make is whether or not to believe that the universe is friendly. Although I can't be sure he actually spoke these words, I've got to believe that only a genius such as Einstein could pack so much wisdom into one sentence. First, belief is a choice, a willful decision. Second, no belief is more significant than the way we choose to view our world. And third, the key is not to decide through logic whether the universe is friendly (an impossible task even for a mind like Einstein's) but rather to choose whether we *believe* it to be friendly.

Einstein seemed to go out of his way to accentuate this last point in another statement widely attributed to him — this one about both the way we choose to view the world and how we choose to act in it: "There are only two ways to live your life. One is as though nothing is a miracle. The other is as though everything is a miracle."

I couldn't begin to explain the meaning of Einstein's theory of relativity or even identify the components of his equation $E = mc^2$, but these two quotes, I'm pretty sure I get. I think Einstein is suggesting that there are some things we humans are just not equipped to know, so we must consciously choose what we want to believe about the world and act in accordance with our convictions. Putting all this in the affirmative, I think Einstein, were he alive and giving motivational seminars (now there's an image!), might offer us this advice:

Choose to believe that the universe is friendly and sacred, and choose to live your life with reverence.

This, for me, is the first and most essential step in making belief. It puts the universe squarely on my side in battling doubt and asks nothing of me other than my willingness to affirm that I am part of some fundamentally supportive life system. Just what that system looks like and how it works I don't even pretend to understand; I leave that to the philosophers and religious scholars to debate. For the purposes of making belief, all that matters here is that I choose to see the universe as supporting me to the full extent that I am willing to draw on it, and in ways that serve my Greater Good — that is, my role in an infinitely greater *universal* plan of which I'm a part.

The best analogy I've found for all this comes from one of my favorite books, *The Will to Believe*, by Marcus Bach. In it, Bach asks an endurance swimmer how she can swim for hours on end. She tells him she views the water as her friend, one wanting to help and work with her. As Bach goes on to observe, each of is in the "swim" of life, and because the waves and currents and tides hit us and pull at us from time to time, it's not always easy to remember that the water is friendly. "It requires an act of faith, a volitional act; it means work," Bach says, "but most of all it requires a will to believe." Still, as Bach points out, the more we choose to use this will, the easier it becomes.

This certainly has been my own experience in learning how to make belief, and I am in constant awe of the way the universe has helped me over the years to pursue my own Greater Good, offering up seemingly endless resources for studying the mechanics of belief and sharing them in constructive ways.

STEP 2: EMBRACE THE POSSIBILITY IN EVERY MOMENT

If the universe is friendly and working in support of my Greater Good, then every moment of this life is rich with possibility. Since I am choosing to believe the former proposition, I must also choose to believe the latter. And this is key for anyone stuck in Doubt, mainly because our bullies want us to lose sight of all the possibility in the present moment.

Think about the way that our doubt nemeses use time against us. First, there's the nature of their taunting "what if" questions, most (though not all) of them suggesting we should dwell on what might have happened in the past and what could happen in the future: *What if you hit someone with your car yesterday, Jeff?* (past). *What if your date never calls, Lisa?* (future). *What if you failed to set the school alarm, Mandi?* (past). *What if you stab someone with a knife, Amy?* (future). The more we fixate on the past and future, the more we squander every precious present moment.

And then, of course, there's the matter of lost time when we're stuck in Doubt, looking for exits. It's pretty hard to tap into any kind of present-moment possibility if each of those moments is spent falling through the same trapdoors again and again. Checking, reassurance-seeking, ruminating, protecting, fixing, avoiding: these things eat up time — a lifetime's worth, if we're not careful. I'm reminded of this whenever I see pictures of my daughters from the many years I was lost in Doubt. What I wouldn't give to have that time back again!

So how do we tap into the possibility of each and every moment? The short answer is through the reverential practice of seeking meaning and purpose at every opportunity.

Bestselling author Dan Millman, whose remarkable personal story inspired the feature film *Peaceful Warrior*, likens life to a classroom in which we learn all we need in order to grow. As a former world champion gymnast, martial arts instructor, college professor, university coach, and author of more than a dozen international bestsellers, Millman has certainly proved himself to be one heck of a student, and through his education he has inspired millions of readers, students, and now moviegoers around the world. Is he seeking meaning and purpose in every moment of his life? I'd sure say so.

Dan Millman, by the way, is one of three experts I've asked to help usher us out of the Shadow of Doubt by answering occasional requests for additional "directions" in each of the chapters in this section. Our other two guides are bestselling author Sylvia Boorstein, whose Western interpretations of Buddhist principles offer some of the most practical "power to choose" advice I've ever run across, and the Reverend Michael Moran, cofounder of Spiritual Life Center in Sacramento, California, and one of the nation's leading authorities on interfaith religion. Together these three represent a wealth of wisdom. I'm greatly indebted to each of them, both for the sage advice I've taken from their work in my own recovery and for their willingness to share their insights here.

Ascribing meaning to life is crucial when we're stuck in Doubt — or facing any life challenge, for that matter — because that meaning, that sense of purpose, affords us more motivation than anything else we could possibly draw on. For proof of that, we need look no further than the amazing life and work of Viktor Frankl.

Frankl is widely known as the father of logotherapy, a school of psychology centered on the belief that the primary motivational force for human beings is our search for meaning. The theory itself is rather profound, but for me it's the story behind it that makes it so powerful. Frankl, you see, came up with the idea while a prisoner in Nazi death camps. He observed that those prisoners who believed there was some kind of meaningful task awaiting them were the most likely to survive. For Frankl, that task was reconstructing a manuscript that was confiscated from him on his arrival at Auschwitz, and to that end he began jotting down notes on small scraps of paper. He credits that reconstruction process with keeping him alive through a bout with typhus fever during his days as a prisoner.

Victor Frankl survived incredible odds to pursue his goal of publishing his manuscript, along with many other books. Through his pursuit, he demonstrated the three tenets of his logotherapy philosophy:

- Life has meaning under all circumstances, even the most miserable ones.
- Our main motivation for living is our will to find meaning in life.
- We have freedom to find meaning in what we do and what we experience, or at least in the stand that we take when faced with a situation of unchangeable suffering.

As I've said, and will stress again and again in the coming pages, making belief is tough work. It requires us to face down our fears and doubts and learn to sit with the seemingly unbearable discomfort they cause. It requires us to replace our goal of avoiding discomfort with a more powerful Greater Good goal. Frankl put this notion into words better than anyone else I've run across: "What man actually needs is not a tensionless state but rather the striving and struggling for a worthwhile goal, a freely chosen task. What he needs is not the discharge of tension at any cost but the call of a potential meaning waiting to be fulfilled by him."

Embrace the Greater Good possibility in every moment, I believe Frankl was suggesting, and you can find the strength to do anything. Doubt doesn't stand a chance!

STEP 3: AFFIRM YOUR UNIVERSAL POTENTIAL

I have a dog tag I wear around my neck. It reads "Believer," and I first put it on more than twenty-five years ago, shortly before a cross-country bus trip I took to discover the world. This was during what I've come to call my "normal" years — that small wedge of time between my childhood OCD and my adult OCD. I was young, carefree, and idealistic in those days, and the inscription I had engraved on the pendant was more about my plans to conquer the world than about freeing myself from the confines of Doubt.

In the years that followed, though, as I fell deeper and deeper into the Shadow, that dog tag became a lifeline for me, a reminder that there was more to me than the obsessions and compulsions that seemed to define me. Doubt has a way of gnawing away at your core, and before you know it, you can lose sight of your very identity.

I know today that I am not defined by my "what if" questions — that they are, in fact, manifestations of my faulty brain wiring. I know that I am a person battling OCD, not someone defined only by my disorder. But learning to make that distinction has taken a lot of work. And I know from my outreach that this challenge can be just as tough for non-OCD sufferers who find themselves deep in Doubt. When Sarah Allen Benton began her new life of sobriety, for example, her doubt bully peppered her with questions about who the new Sarah would be and how her friends would perceive her. The more she allowed herself to identify with the questions, the more she forgot her true identity.

So who is the real Sarah? Who is the real me? The real you? Those are deep questions, for sure, and the answers, I'm certain, are far more profound than I am capable of offering. I do know one thing, though: if we choose to see the universe as friendly and work-ing to help each of us pursue our Greater Good, then each of us, as a part of this universe, must have an identity bigger than we know — one that has the full potential of the universe available to it. I must be far more powerful, more capable, more grand than I rec-ognize — certainly much more so than my doubt bully would have me believe.

Think for a moment about an acorn: it has inside it a mighty oak tree. Or a caterpillar: inside it is a magnificent butterfly. So it is, I believe, with each of us. And while I don't pretend to understand what our true human identities are, I know what they aren't. I know they are not merely our doubts and fears. Affirming this simple truth is crucial in making belief, and so too is affirming our universal poten-tial. This is an ongoing challenge, and the key lies in recognizing and calling out our identity-robbing doubts — a process I find greatly facilitated by the practice of mindfulness.

I have only a rudimentary understanding of the principles of mindfulness, but the more I learn about them, the more I find myself able to sort out what's what in my doubt-infested head. At its core, mindfulness is about concentrating one's awareness on the present moment and observing, dispassionately, the constant stream of thoughts that ensue. The power of this practice lies in the opportunity it presents to strip emotions from the maelstrom of thoughts swirling between our ears. Or, as Sylvia Boorstein puts it: "Mindfulness doesn't erase confusion as much as it notices it and dissolves, or at least reduces, the fear about it."

Because of the unique laboratory it presents, OCD has become an increasingly popular research topic for scientists and others looking to explore the mind-brain connection — that is, the correlations and distinctions between one's thoughts and one's "inner thinker" of those thoughts. Brain scientist Dr. Jeffrey Schwartz and science writer Sharon Begley tackle these issues in *The Mind and the Brain*, offering some powerful conclusions about the role that mindful awareness can play in combating obsessions and compulsions; and as Schwartz has long advocated, the simple practice of relabeling both components is key.

As esoteric as the whole practice of mindfulness might seem, its application in making belief actually couldn't be easier. Here are a couple of examples:

I am walking down a street when I inadvertently kick a small rock. Before I even know it, my bully is hitting me with a barrage of "what if" questions: *What if a barefooted kid steps on that rock and cuts his foot because of where you've moved it? What if that kid then bleeds to death?* And so on. In the old days, I might have immediately headed for the trapdoor of protecting and stooped down to pick up the rock, never even realizing that I was feeding my doubt monster and again reinforcing the OCD cycle.

Today, instead, I can typically call out my doubt bully just as he begins his act. As soon as the "what ifs" start, I simply label the questions as obsessions, saying out loud (or silently, if there are people around me), "I am obsessing about what might happen because of that rock." Likewise, instead of blindly following my bully to the protecting trapdoor, I can label this impulse as one leading to a compulsion: "I am fighting the compulsive urge to pick up and remove that rock because my bully suggests someone could get hurt if I don't." Just like that, I have introduced a layer of mindful awareness into the equation, and in so doing, I have robbed my bully of much of his power.

This same process is effective for the most common everyday fear-based doubts. Take my friend Lisa and her post-date agony. As Lisa sat in her office the day after her date, wondering why her male friend hadn't called and checking her answering machine hour after hour, she could have gained some leverage in battling her doubt bully simply by calling him out. "I am mulling over all kinds of fear-based doubts surrounding why he hasn't called," she might have said to herself. "And I am fighting the urge to reduce my anxiety by checking the answering machine." Or, put another way: "I see what you're doing to me, Mr. Bully!"

Mindfulness can't, in and of itself, remind us of our true nature, but it can clear the way for us to recognize it. By calling out our fear-based doubts, we reinforce the fact that they neither comprise nor define us. They are simply thoughts, meaningless except for the meaning that we assign them. And whatever part of me that is capable of observing this — my inner believer, for lack of a better term — is also capable of tapping into the full potential of the friendly universe (that is, my universal potential). I need only to affirm this.

Of course, to do this consistently, we need a whole lot of *resolve*.

ON MINDFULNESS IN OCD TREATMENT

Jeffrey Schwartz, MD, coauthor of *The Mind and the Brain*

Q: **How did you come to recommend that OCD sufferers relabel their obsessions and compulsions?**

A: I basically took these ideas from what I had learned doing Theravada Buddhist meditation. This practice is essentially a very user-friendly, very grounded, very practical way for people with OCD to apply a Buddhist philosophy meditation technique called "making a mental note," or relabeling. The concept of mindful awareness was developed by Gotama, the Buddha, as a tool for eliminating suffering. His message was that if you use this awareness technique, this mindful-observation approach, you will be able to alleviate suffering by decreasing the craving that your material aspects of yourself cause you to become attached to. Interestingly, I've recently come to realize that one can very effectively apply the same techniques using a Christian perspective.

Q: **Do you see empirical evidence that mindfulness is effective in decreasing suffering?**

A: There's a lot of scientific data, collected in the last five years, that shows that when you relabel something, it markedly enhances a frontal cortex area, mainly the lower aspect of the prefrontal cortex; and, through a circuit, that process decreases activity in an emotional part of the brain called the amygdala. So there's now evidence that putting labels on thoughts causes the front cortex to modulate the emotional brain. That's very understandable in terms of what's been known since ancient times about "impartial spectators" and mindful awareness.

ON LIVING WITH PURPOSE

Dan Millman, bestselling author of *Way of the Peaceful Warrior*

Q: You have described our world as a "divine school" and daily life as a "classroom." How has this framework served you in dealing with adversity?

A: Life arises, moment to moment, out of mystery. Nothing [innately] means anything. We humans create our own meanings, positive or negative, and add concepts and complications, labels and categories, in a brave attempt to make sense and order out of this beautiful, random world. So, to create meaning and sense, I choose to view the world as a school, and the challenges of life as ways, or paths, to personal growth. If we are here for fun or pleasure or wealth, then anything that threatens these qualities becomes a negative. But if we are here to learn and evolve, then even adversity serves this great purpose. I have chosen a worldview that provides positive meaning and purpose, this understanding that the challenges of daily life are forms of spiritual weight lifting to strengthen our spirits and forge our character.

Q: You have written often about seeking meaning and purpose in every moment. In what ways does this practice serve us?

A: Author and fellow quotation-collector Robert Byrne once said, "The purpose of life is a life of purpose." I have already addressed how we create our meanings. But this matter of purpose appears, moment to moment, in our lives. Many of us want to discover — to mentally know with certainty — our "purpose in life." I have addressed this larger question in several of my books, including *Living on Purpose*. And in a forthcoming book, *The Four Purposes of Life*, I will

continued ↘

present a clear map to address the larger picture. Meanwhile, if we each focus on our purpose that arises in front of us, in each moment, this enhances the quality of each moment, and thus the quality of our life.

ON MINDFULNESS

Sylvia Boorstein, author of *It's Easier Than You Think*

Q: You write in *It's Easier Than You Think* that "the ability to sustain attention in the truth of the moment is the antidote to doubt." Do you think this is connected to our doubt bullies' efforts to keep us worrying about what happened in the past and what might happen in the future (at the expense of this moment)?

A: I think that when my mind is steady, when I put myself in the truth of this moment, specifically about worries about the future and concerns about the past, I'm able to see that *this* is a worry about the future, *this* is a concern about the past; *this* is not what's happening now. What's happening now is not those things. What's happening now is that doubt has arisen in my mind, making these thoughts; and the truth of the moment is that my doubt mechanism has popped into action.

Q: In what way is this helpful in confronting doubt?

A: When I see this in myself — "Oh, suppose this or suppose that [will happen]" — I think to myself, This is your fear response popping into action, this is your "tape" about catastrophic possibilities. This is not the truth of what's happening. And that actually brings my attention back to the present. It keeps me from squandering the pleasure of being in this present moment, in which we can do what we need to do.

ON RELIGION AND "TRUE NATURE"

Rev. Michael Moran,
cofounder of Spiritual Life Center in Sacramento, California

Q: You have long been a student of world religions. What common threads do you find when it comes to their descriptions of our true nature and universal potential?

A: The very intent of most of the great religions of the world is to awaken their followers to the awesome power of God. The Hindus tell a story that the gods hid humankind's divine nature in the last place they would ever think to look — within themselves. The Hindus reverently greet each other with "Namaste," which translates as "The divine within me greets and bows to the divine in you." In this way they remind themselves that all of life is sacred. The Torah begins by telling us that we are created in the image and after the likeness of God, and that all of creation is good. The image the writer of Genesis shares is of God breathing his life into man. In the New Testament, that inner power is beautifully referenced in 2 Timothy 1:7: "For God did not give us a spirit of fear, but one of power, love and self-discipline." Buddhism states that through the power of thought, one can achieve one's true nature — Buddha nature.

Q: Why the need for all these reminders?

A: Too often we identify with our lower nature or small ego self. By doing this, we limit our ability to experience and express the goodness of life. We suffer needlessly.

KEY POINTS

- In standing up to our doubt bullies, we must learn to believe in ourselves, in others, and in life.
- This process involves four key principles:
  - ✳ reverence
  - ✳ resolve
  - ✳ investment
  - ✳ surrender
- To implement these four principles, we can take ten simple steps that offer a way out when stuck in Doubt.
- Applying the principle of reverence involves taking three steps:
  - ✳ **Step 1. Choose to see the universe as friendly.**

    Recognize that you are free to choose what you believe about the universe.

    Affirm that the universe is working to help you pursue your Greater Good.
  - ✳ **Step 2. Embrace the possibility in every moment.**

    Choose to see life as a classroom offering lessons at every turn.

    Seek meaning and purpose in every situation.

    Allow your Greater Good goals to motivate you.
  - ✳ **Step 3. Affirm your universal potential.**

    Recognize that you, as part of a universe with infinite potential, must also have that potential inside.

    Allow mindfulness to help you call out your doubt bully's "what if" questions and demands.

    Recognize that the part of you that is capable of observing your thoughts is also capable of tapping into the full potential of the universe.

CHAPTER FIVE

Resolve

Second Principle of Making Belief

I f Steps 1, 2, and 3 of the making-belief process point us in the right direction for escaping Doubt, then the next two aim to keep us from turning back. They are the steps we need to take when our sense of reverence is tested — as it will be again and again. And they are arguably the toughest steps. Affirming that we are each part of a friendly, supportive universe offering us boundless possibility is crucial, for sure; but without the resolve to keep that frame of mind when we're challenged, our affirmations are hollow and get us nowhere.

With that as background, I should probably interject a small confession here (though perhaps it should have been plastered in bold letters across the front cover): if you picked up this book looking for easy solutions for dealing with uncertainty, well, I'm afraid you're out of luck. The approach I'm advocating works; I know this from firsthand experience. But it's far from easy. In fact, I can honestly say it represents some of the toughest and most painful work I've ever had to do. But . . . have I mentioned that it works? It *really works!*

STEP 4: PUT YOUR COMMITMENTS AHEAD OF YOUR COMFORT

Okay, then, those of you whom I didn't just scare off, allow me to reward you with the single greatest truth about uncertainty that I know:

The key to living with uncertainty is learning to embrace the discomfort of uncertainty.

"Huh?!" I hear you protesting. "I paid $14.95 for this?"

Before you fire off a note to me demanding your money back, please read on and take in the words of a writer much wiser than I — one who has devoted her life to exploring the concept of uncertainty. They are the words of the American Buddhist nun Pema Chödrön, who wrote: "The central question . . . is not how we avoid uncertainty and fear but how we relate to discomfort." She goes on: "Sticking with uncertainty is how we learn to relax in the midst of chaos, how we learn to be cool when the ground beneath us suddenly disappears."

For those of us stuck in Doubt, it would seem the "chaos" to which Pema refers is the cacophony of "what if " questions bouncing around our heads, and the "disappearing ground beneath us" could very well be the opening of one of our many alluring trapdoors. To be able to "relax" and "be cool" when in this predicament would be huge. Right?

All together: Right!

But Pema says we need to stick with the uncertainty, to sit with its discomfort. And that is the *last* thing we want to do. Right?

Right! But here's the thing: it seems Pema has not just Buddhist philosophy on her side, but also the full weight of science. Study after study has shown that the most effective way to decrease the discomfort of uncertainty is to habituate ourselves to it through direct exposure. This, in fact, is the very key to the exposure/response-prevention treatment for OCD that I described earlier. I could point you toward all kinds of charts and figures that document its efficacy, but suffice it to say that the effectiveness of this desensitization process is scientific fact. And therein lies both the good news and the bad.

Let's consider what Step 4 means for our Shadow of Doubt tour guides. Andy, I'm afraid, is going to have to sit with the possibility that his doctors may indeed have missed something. Jared, when faced with questions about his potential negligence, is going to have to consider the prospect that he has, in fact, created a hazard. Terry needs to accept that maybe she was indeed out of line in her comments to her friend. Lisa, I'm sorry to say, is going to have to consider the possibility that her date is just not interested in seeing her again. Carole needs to make peace with the reality that her repeating rituals can't ensure her daughter's safety. Sarah must accept that she may very well lose some friends because of her sobriety. Matt and Samantha are both going to have to understand that some things may never feel right. Amy will have to accept that there's no way to completely convince herself that she can be trusted around knives. And Mandi needs to embrace the inevitable uncertainty that comes with engaging in life.

Ouch!

Pretty tough prescriptions — and these are for people I call friends. (Imagine my advice for folks I don't like!) Yet what are the alternatives? Andy could check, Jared and Tammy could seek reassurance, Carole could go through her protecting rituals, and so on. But we've already seen where those trapdoors got them.

The cold, hard truth is that if our tour guides really want to find their way out of the Shadow of Doubt — if they are willing to make that commitment — then they must resolve to put that commitment ahead of their comfort, no matter how difficult that might be.

STEP 5: KEEP SIGHT OF THE BIG PICTURE
AND THE GREATER GOOD

Step 4 represents what I've come to think of as the "tough love" approach to addressing uncertainty. It is, as I've stressed, at the very core of traditional OCD therapy, and for years my own therapist drove this point home. I heard her message week after week. I understood the principle. But, as I confess in *Rewind, Replay, Repeat*, I did little more than pay lip service to the whole approach during those years: I merely went through the motions during therapy sessions and frequently lied about having completed my exposure homework assignments in between. Why? After all, I was paying a lot of money for those sessions!

The short answer is that the then-best-available treatment approaches had taught me *how* to get better, but not *why*. I had been given strategies for confronting my doubt, but not for finding the motivation to do so. This was fifteen years ago, and the field of psychology had not yet begun in earnest to address the many issues surrounding treatment motivation. Today this is a hot area of clinical and academic research — and I'll get back to it shortly — but in the early nineties, I was largely on my own.

It was out of necessity, really, that I began seeking out ways to motivate myself, searching mostly for frameworks larger than my own myopic view from the Shadow. I became a voracious reader of self-help, motivational, and applied spirituality books. I devoured the works of Dan Millman, Marianne Williamson, Wayne Dyer, Richard Bach, Emmet Fox, Gerald Jampolsky, Norman Vincent Peale, and Stephen Covey. I sat in on countless worship services and motivational seminars. I became a vicarious student of the twelve-step recovery model, learning its principles through a number of friends who shared with me what they had discovered.

From all my research, I started piecing together a view of that friendly universe Albert Einstein prompted me to consider — a universe that mystified me in all ways but one: I knew it begged a much bigger picture of things than the dark and dingy ones my doubt bully was painting for me. I hadn't a clue what this bigger picture looked like, but by simply allowing myself to consider its existence, I found myself shifting my perspective in increasingly constructive ways.

The first of these shifts was a rather silly one. Literally. Throughout my "normal" years, I always had a healthy sense of humor. I liked practical jokes, funny movies, witty books, good stand-up comedy, laughing out loud, cracking up others. I had a knack for not taking life too seriously, and so did Samantha. Our dating days and the early years of our marriage were filled with laughter.

That, however, changed almost overnight in the mid-nineties, when my world started spinning out of control and I landed smack-dab in the middle of the Shadow of Doubt, a very humorless place. Plagued by my bully's taunting, and falling through trapdoors all around me, I simply stopped laughing. Lost in the darkness, along with so much of my identity, was that sense of humor that had served me so well.

Fortunately for me, both my therapist and my wife were relentless in their quest to help me see the absurdity of my OCD patterns, with Samantha going so far as to write catchy little ditties about my compulsive checking for victims of my unwitting negligence:

I killed a man in Frisco,
One in Oakland too.
Dead bodies, they surround me,
Oh, what am I to do?

Most of the time, her playful prodding just annoyed me. But occasionally I couldn't help laughing, and when I did, it was almost as if my bully just disappeared   poof. I wasn't really sure what to make of that, but I had to admit that it worked and that it seemed to confirm one of the recurring themes in all my big-picture research. From the tenets of Judaism, Christianity, and Buddhism, to the themes of the self-help and applied spirituality books I was reading, the message was clear: try not to take life too seriously.

I share this here because I want more than anything through this book to offer practical solutions, and this nugget of wisdom from the school of hard knocks is as practical as they get: practice laughing! If it helps to know that the universe itself has a sense of humor (and that if you look for it, you'll find it everywhere), then allow me to share my favorite proof of this — in the form of an email I got shortly after *Rewind, Replay, Repeat* was published.

"Hi Jeff," it began. "As a regular listener to KCBS, I was very interested in reading your book and purchased it last week." (Ah, another fan letter. How nice.) "As I was reading it, though, all of a sudden things didn't seem to make sense," the note went on. "It seemed like it just jumped around." (Uh oh! This reader is about to rip apart my writing.) "I kept reading, though, and suddenly realized I was reading a chapter for the second time."

Huh?

"It seems my copy of the book skipped from page 80 to 127 and then repeated pages 127 forward again later in the book." (Yikes!) The reader explained that she'd returned the book to the store where she'd bought it and that the other copies in stock had the same defect. In a panic, I fired off notes to my publisher and agent.

Several days and many phone calls later, my book team was able to trace the problem to a single box of books that had somehow been bound incorrectly. Just sixty of the twenty thousand printed copies had gone out to stores missing pages — a mere 0.3 percent. Still, it wasn't long before I started hearing from readers scattered throughout the United States. I was crestfallen, embarrassed, frustrated, and anxious.

But then the irony hit me: What were the chances? Yes, these things occasionally happen in the publishing world — but very infrequently, according to both my editor and agent, neither of whom had ever had to deal with this particular problem during their long careers. "Of all books to have an 'order' issue," each was quick to point out, "it had to be a book about OCD!" The irony wasn't lost on the readers who notified me, either, several of whom went out of their way to apologize for having to share what must be very tough news for someone with OCD.

The more I saw the absurdity of it, the more I was able to step back and see the humor. The universe was winking at me, I decided, and the story became a great icebreaker in my talks and interviews. I even tracked down one of the "special" books to keep as a memento.

Regaining my sense of humor has been one of the most rewarding aspects of my OCD recovery; but, like every other aspect of this recovery process, it takes work. I take very seriously my commitment to not taking life too seriously. I go out of my way to find reasons to laugh. Oly helps me a lot on this front.

Oly is a gift that a colleague brought me back from New York shortly after *Rewind, Replay, Repeat* was published. "I have something for you," she'd said, as she handed me a bag. "I'm a little afraid, though, that you might be offended."

As you can imagine, I opened the bag with some trepidation. Inside, though, was one of the best gifts I've ever received: a five-and-a-quarter-inch "Obsessive Compulsive Action Figure," beautifully packaged with a surgical mask; sanitary, hypoallergenic moist towelette; and detailed daily itinerary, with such items as "8:33 p.m. — Brushes teeth, disposes of toothbrush." Oly, as I've nicknamed my little friend, has crisscrossed the country with me over the past couple of years, becoming both a crowd-pleasing prop in my talks and an indispensable personal reminder to keep my sense of humor.

Finding the humor in life may seem like an unlikely strategy for making belief, but I've come to see it as a means to an end — a way of breaking out of the myopic view from the Shadow. Much like standing under the stars at night or staring out over a mighty ocean, it offers the power of a constructive perspective shift, an invaluable tool for staying the course when our resolve is tested.

Keeping sight of the big picture goes a long way toward providing the inner strength necessary to put our commitments ahead of our comfort. But it's only half the process. The other half requires that we identify for ourselves specific ways in which we can pursue our Greater Good — that is, ways in which we can be of *service* to others or enhance our own sense of *purpose*. We'll explore this practice, and its role in decision making, in much greater detail in chapter 8. To keep us moving out of the Shadow, though, I want to stress a few key points here about this notion of Greater Good, starting with the term itself.

First, it's important to note that we're not talking about a Greatest Good. That would defeat the whole purpose: our doubt bullies would have a field day taunting us about whether we could be sure action A, and not action B, was truly the greatest possible good we could be pursuing at any given moment. The bullies would be making a valid point! I personally don't believe we mortals are endowed with the ability to make such a distinction. That said, though, I also believe that each and every moment presents us with infinite ways to be of service and enhance our own sense of purpose, any one of which becomes a Greater Good relative to the perceived "good" that Doubt's trapdoors have to offer. (Please note that, moving forward, I will put *good* and *bad* in quotes when they are my bully's designations, not my own.)

Let's go back to my example from the last chapter. I'm walking down the street when I inadvertently kick a small rock and start obsessing about the horrific things that might happen as a result. My bully does his best to convince me that the "good" thing to do would be to pick up the rock so no one can get hurt. Practicing mindfulness, I call out the obsession and compulsion for what they are and keep walking, doing my best to ignore my doubt bully's taunting. My distress builds, and my bully reminds me of the relief I would get by returning to the rock and picking it up. No, I tell myself, what I need to do is sit with this anxiety. But how? The distress is building and building.

This is where I need to identify a Greater Good, something to trump the "good" my bully is offering. Let's say I'm on my way to work as all this is unfolding. Doubling back to pick up the rock would take time and would likely make me late getting to the radio station. People are counting on me there, and I can best be of service to them by arriving on time. Even more important, I know that standing up to my doubt bully here is an opportunity to further my recovery and thus enhance my sense of purpose by pursuing my full potential outside the Shadow. Reminding myself of this "good" versus Greater Good relativity provides an immensely powerful motivator for confronting doubt.

I want to conclude this chapter by sharing a quick overview of a motivational concept known as acceptance and commitment therapy, or ACT. I must confess that before tackling this book project, I knew very little about ACT, but the term kept coming up in my outreach, mostly in conversations with OCD experts who pointed out the parallels between my approach to finding motivation and the principles of ACT.

Out of curiosity, I began looking into ACT and its practical application, turning first to the bestselling book on the topic, *Get Out of Your Mind and Into Your Life: The New Acceptance and Commitment Therapy*, by Dr. Steven Hayes, often seen as the "father" of ACT. From reading just the opening paragraphs, I could see why people so often asked if I was familiar with Hayes's work. The motivational approach he so methodically and scientifically lays out is indeed very much in line with the framework that I, as a layperson in need, developed for myself; in fact, the parallels are uncanny. I find it fascinating that the principles I stumbled into out of necessity fit so well into a framework as scientifically sound (exhaustively researched, applied, and tested) as the one Hayes has developed.

In a nutshell, ACT employs three categories of techniques: mindfulness, acceptance, and values-based living. Through mindfulness, clients learn to examine their pain and see the world from beyond the vantage point of that pain. Acceptance involves drawing distinctions between pain and suffering and choosing to accept (rather than trying to avoid or eliminate) the pain. And values-based living involves having ACT clients identify what they most want from life and then use those values to guide their decision making.

Hayes's framework strikes me as much more holistic and broad-based than my own model, which offers strategies for making belief in moments of critical decision making. However, the underlying principles are indeed very similar.

ON ACCEPTANCE AND COMMITMENT THERAPY

Steven Hayes, PhD, author of *Get Out of Your Mind and Into Your Life*

Q: The term *acceptance* can have a negative connotation for some people who take it to mean rolling over and giving up when challenged. That's not the kind of active acceptance that you are advocating, is it?

A: That's right. The kind of acceptance we're talking about is really a matter of embracing the moment, of reaching out and feeling what there is to be felt — to be inside your skin, experiencing what you're experiencing. What we're talking

continued ⤳

about is a moment-to-moment embrace of what is, as it is, not as what it says it is. We're not asking you to accept that you are contaminating others, or that you are a bad person, or that you are going to die from a panic attack. We're asking you to experience feeling what it's like to be with those thoughts, memories, and bodily sensations.

Q: Personally, I have found that two motivators — service and purpose — are more powerful for me than any others. I call them my Greater Good. How would ACT describe this approach? From your perspective, what have I done in developing this framework?

A: I think what you're finding is that if you're going to do something other than what your mind tells you to do, what your emotions tell you to do, you're going to have to find a conscious part of you making choices about what you want to do. And when you choose to do what you really care about, especially things that establish something meaningful right here in the present, that gives you a kind of vitality and flexibility and a positive purpose that will allow you to walk through the hell of your own history. And a lot of people who struggle have some really difficult things to walk through, so the short and quick way to say it is that the positive will outweigh negative any day, if you can find a way to connect with it. These positive, meaningful, purpose-driven kinds of experiences — what I want to be about, what I'm up to, how I want to spend my seconds on this planet — these are a sort of lighthouse in the distance, a guide. So, I think what you're finding is that positive, purposeful, goal-directed, values-based actions have a kind of gentle pull that is very flexible: if one way is not working, try some other way.

ON DISCOMFORT

Dan Millman

Q: As a world-class gymnast, you had to push through a lot of pain. Talk, if you would, about the role of discomfort in pursuing one's potential.

A: Thomas Edison once wrote, "Most people miss opportunity because it's dressed in overalls and looks like work." I've observed that most people grow through effort over time — through stretching our limits, just as we do in physical exercise. We don't get more flexible, or stronger, unless we push past our comfort zone. As I clarify in *Body Mind Mastery*, life develops what it demands. No demand, no development. I am not, however, a believer in "no pain, no gain." The secret is to balance pleasure and pain. This sense of balance is key not only in gymnastics, but in every facet of life.

ON COMPASSION

Sylvia Boorstein

Q: You frequently stress the importance of compassion in keeping sight of the big picture. What advice can you offer for exercising one's compassion?

A: Here's a practice that anyone can do — in an airplane or on a bus, sitting in a conference room with people talking, anywhere: Look around and think to yourself, I only know the outside stories of any of these people. I don't know who of these people has a partner who is dying, or has just miscarried

continued ⮑

their third pregnancy, or has just heard news that they might lose their job, or whose mother is sick, or who at this moment is in terrible pain because they have just given up cigarettes, or they have just gone to AA, or they have just decided to overcome their compulsive need to check, or something else. I don't know who suffers from what. I know that I have my own baggage that I carry around from one meeting and one train and one bus to the next, and everybody's carrying their own. The more that I feel my own, the more that I know that everyone's got something. If I had magical eyes, I could see what people are carrying in their backpack of troubles, and this would inspire two things in me: compassion for both myself and other people, and a real sense of goodwill for them at the same time, because I think we are all heroic. Everyone who is sitting around that conference table or that bus or that airplane got out of bed that morning and put on their socks and went out of their house. That's a heroic act.

ON PUTTING COMMITMENTS AHEAD OF COMFORT

Rev. Michael Moran

Q: Much of what I've learned about putting commitments ahead of comfort comes from lessons you've offered over the years. What can you share here about the importance of this life strategy?

A: Many years ago a mentor cautioned me that if my plans and dreams were not lofty enough to make my knees knock, they were too small and not worthy of my time and effort. I have found this to be true. The things in my life for which I am

continued ⤳

most grateful seemed beyond impossible at first thought. They took me far out of my comfort zone and brought up every fear, doubt, and sense of inadequacy within me. To accomplish them, I had to face my inner demons, risk the humiliation of failure, and find an inner resolve that I only hoped was there. The beautiful Twenty-third Psalm has helped millions of people for thousands of years to persevere during many long, dark nights of the soul. It offers some of the best advice I have ever heard for dealing with those frightening times: "Even though I walk through the valley of the shadow of death, I will fear no evil, for You are with me." Did you notice the author encouraged us to keep walking, keep moving, to rely on the power of God within us, and whatever we do, don't stop when going through hellish times?

Q: I've also heard you point to the civil rights movement as evidence of this.

A: Yes. A famous civil rights–era singer (Mavis Staples, of the Staple Singers) talked about the high price demanded to gain civil rights for black Americans during those turbulent times. She reported that Dr. Martin Luther King Jr. and the other civil rights leaders kept the Freedom Marchers motivated by telling them the hard truth that much would be asked of them, there would be great struggle and pain, and they would have to walk through "hell" before they achieved their noble cause.... Dr. King, following the lead of his mentor, Mahatma Gandhi, constantly reminded the Freedom Marchers that their true natures would be revealed not during the easy, comfortable times but in the midst of all the hardship, uncertainty, and controversy. He told them to dig deep within themselves, keep their faith in God, and never, never to take their eyes off the prize.

KEY POINTS

- Applying the principle of resolve involves taking the following steps:
    - ✳ **Step 4. Put your commitments ahead of your comfort.**

      The key to living with uncertainty is learning to embrace the discomfort of uncertainty.

      This strategy is supported both by ancient philosophies and by recent scientific studies.

      This strategy is also at the heart of traditional OCD therapy (exposure/response-prevention, or ERP therapy) and relies on the phenomenon of habituation, which causes the discomfort of anxiety to decrease over time.

    - ✳ **Step 5. Keep sight of the big picture and the Greater Good.**

      This strategy aims to help you find the motivation for what's asked of you in Step 4.

      Finding and employing your sense of humor is a powerful means of keeping sight of the big picture.

      Identifying Greater Good goals involves finding ways in which to be of service to other people or enhance your own sense of purpose.

- Acceptance and commitment therapy (ACT) is a motivational process employing three techniques:
    - ✳ Mindfulness: looking at your pain.
    - ✳ Acceptance: embracing your pain in a constructive way.
    - ✳ Values-based living: identifying motivating values and using those values to make constructive decisions.

CHAPTER SIX

Investment

Third Principle of Making Belief

I want next to introduce you to Director Doubt. If you've read *Rewind, Replay, Repeat*, you've already met my personal doubt bully; if you've watched the movie *The Truman Show*, then you've seen him in action.

My doubt nemesis is Ed Harris, or more accurately, Christof, the character Harris plays in this brilliant Peter Weir film. Christof is the eccentric director of a reality TV program called *The Truman Show*, in which hundreds of cameras — and millions of viewers — follow the show's unwitting star, Truman Burbank, through every moment of his life. Poor Truman has no idea that all the people around him are hired actors or that he is living in a mammoth studio bubble. He thinks he's on an island. It's Christof's job to make sure that Truman doesn't discover the truth.

I was sitting in a theater shortly after this movie's release, watching Christof devise one trap after another (fires, storms, and so on) to keep the ever-curious Truman from venturing too far from his soundstage home, playing off Truman's fears at every turn, when I suddenly realized that this was *exactly* how my doubt bully functioned. Much like Christof, my Director Doubt was doing all he could to secure his own job, setting traps to keep me stuck in Doubt, directing my life through fear and uncertainty. And I was letting him! As Christof proclaims in one especially powerful scene in the movie, he is able to control Truman's life only because Truman, not knowing better, allows him to "direct" it.

The next three steps in making belief aim to help us direct those aspects of our own lives that are within our control, and thus allow us to challenge the false realities presented to us and venture out into the unknown, as Truman ultimately chooses to do.

STEP 6: CLAIM AND EXERCISE YOUR FREEDOM TO CHOOSE

Of the countless self-help books I've read over the years, the one that has had the most profound impact on my life is Stephen Covey's classic *The Seven Habits of Highly Effective People*. From Dr. Covey I learned numerous strategies for *investing* in my life, the most fundamental of which is to tap the power of proactivity — that is, to practice willfully inserting our freedom to choose between the stimuli we're confronted with and our responses to them. We, as humans, are endowed with independent will, and so we have the ability to choose. Always. The problem is that we tend to forget this freedom, over and over again. And for those of us with self-preserving doubt bullies, the challenge is that much greater. As Covey points out, the key is to employ and develop our independent will, along with our other human endowments of self-awareness, imagination, and conscience.

So what does this freedom mean for our decision making while stuck in Doubt? Let's revisit a couple of examples, starting with

Carole and her compulsive urges to pick up grocery items from the floor and return them in precise sequences to their proper store shelves.

The stimulus to act here is the anxiety Carole's bully creates by taunting her with suggestions that her daughter's safety is at risk. *What if you fail to protect Frankie by incorrectly returning the box to the shelf?* The response her bully is looking for is Carole's traditional repeating compulsion, one Carole has defaulted to so many times in the past that she often doesn't even question the need to do it. As Christof gloats at one point in *The Truman Show*, we all tend to accept the reality with which we're presented, and Carole's Director Doubt has become so skilled at presenting her with (false) realities about her ability to protect Frankie that she often takes them at face value.

But what if Carole were to insert her freedom to choose in between her version of Director Doubt and the repeating compulsion he wants her to perform? First, she could use her self-awareness to recognize the trap she's about to fall into (perhaps labeling her obsession and compulsion) to call out her bully. Next, she could employ her imagination to consider not acting on the compulsion. Using her conscience, Carole could remind herself of the relative "good" and Greater Good of her two options. And, finally, Carole could rely on her independent will to *choose* not to perform her repeating pattern.

Stephen Covey's proactive model can be just as effective in confronting even the most mundane fear-based doubts — say, Mandi's concern about being overly cautious while making left turns onto busy streets without signals. Here, Mandi's anxiety (the stimulus) prompts her to avoid these situations altogether (her default response). Instead, Mandi could use her self-awareness to see that she is avoiding many otherwise convenient routes strictly because of the anxiety they provoke; she could use her imagination to see herself making the left turns; she could employ her conscience to remind herself of the Greater Good of reclaiming her time lost in taking detours (and giving that extra time to her family, for example); and ultimately she could put her independent will to use, *choosing* to make these left turns.

In the above examples, Carole and Mandi are both tested by their doubt bullies and face them down by exercising their freedom to choose. Because of the difficulty of doing this, they — and anyone else who struggles with uncertainty — would do well to get some practice in between their tests, much as soldiers go through drills again and again, so that they are prepared when tested in battle. As we know from OCD treatment, it's not enough simply to exercise our freedom to choose; we need to actively develop it. This is the principle behind exposure/response-prevention therapy.

I remember many a conversation with my therapist during the early days of my treatment in which I protested her insistence on my doing exposure exercises. "Life already gives me plenty of opportunities to fight my compulsions," I would argue. She would remind me then that those opportunities don't always provide the chance to maximize the benefit of ERP — by sitting with the anxiety that they trigger until that anxiety can dissipate. She was right. If I ran over a pothole on my way to work, for example, I might successfully fight the compulsion to loop my car around for a check of the street. I might also still be highly charged with anxiety when I got to the station. But once at work, chances were good that I'd be distracted fairly quickly by the demands of my job. This distraction certainly helped me get through my day. Unfortunately, though, the natural course of this kind of episode doesn't provide the therapeutic effect of anxiety habituation.

To be clear, I'm not suggesting that every time our doubt bullies get the best of us, we should lock ourselves in a room and sit with the discomfort of their "what if" questions. That's hardly practical and certainly no way to live! I'm only pointing out what the ERP specialists like to hammer home: it's not enough to tackle our doubt challenges as they come; we have to deliberately expose ourselves to them in constructive ways. Carole, for example, might work with a thera-pist to develop a hierarchy of challenges in which she is exposed to triggers that prompt her to indulge her repeating compulsions and then willfully chooses not to do so, while sitting with the discomfort that her restraint creates. And Mandi? She's been around me long enough to know what her homework assignment would be. In fact, it was with great pride that she told me just the other day that she had gone out of her way to turn left onto Highway 12 (without a signal), "just to practice."

This exercising of our free will is a form of training, no different really from what athletes do in between their big games. It's often extremely uncomfortable, but it also offers us endless opportunities to invest in ourselves.

STEP 7: PICTURE POSSIBILITY AND "DIRECT" YOUR ATTENTION

In addition to his proactive "freedom to choose" model, Stephen Covey offers a second investment strategy in *The Seven Habits of Highly Effective People* that has had a profound impact on my approach to life: "Begin with the end in mind."

This concept, as Covey explains it, stems from the notion that we create everything twice — once mentally, and the second time physically. Covey offers the example of building a home, which you certainly wouldn't do without first creating in your own mind all the details and putting them onto paper in the form of construction plans. For obvious reasons, this blueprint analogy resonates strongly with me.

Looking back on my Crash Course in Believing, that year I spent studying and writing about the mechanics of belief, I can now see just how and why the process unfolded so effectively. First, I did, in fact, begin with the end in mind. In contrast to my reactive approach to just about everything in those days, in this case I willfully pictured the possibility of my going public with a success story about recovering from the worst of OCD — despite the fact that I did not yet have any successes to share. I also came up with a detailed plan to make that happen: I would reconnect with my therapist with a new commitment to do the hard work of ERP, and I would take notes on everything. The more I pictured what I could do, the more specific my planning became. I pictured myself learning to believe beyond my constant doubts, and soon enough I had my own set of building plans — a blueprint, if you will — that I then employed to make belief.

Again with the benefit of hindsight, I think this example also serves to point out the interconnectedness of the various steps in this process of making belief. I was able to choose to picture the possibility of my book (Steps 6 and 7) only because I had first chosen to see the universe as supporting me in this effort (Steps 1, 2, and 3) and because I had opted to put this Greater Good goal ahead of my own comfort (Steps 4 and 5). Keeping sight of these objectives is often no easy task, and that's where the second half of Step 7 comes in.

"Look where you are going," philosopher Emmet Fox wrote, "because you will inevitably go where you are looking. Where your attention is, there is your destiny." I admire just about everything Fox ever wrote, but this particular observation is priceless. In two short sentences, Fox takes the concept of picturing possibility one critical step further by calling out the importance of attention and where it takes us.

- Are you looking where you are going?
- Are you giving your attention to the destiny you seek?

I know that when I'm stuck in Doubt, my own answer to each of these questions is always a resounding No.

Think about how things typically work when we're in the Shadow of Doubt: It's dark. We're uncomfortable. We want a quick escape from the discomfort. Our bullies lure us to trapdoors, and because we're not looking where we're going, we fall in, only to become more deeply trapped in the darkness.

Q: Where is our attention during all of this?

A: On the goal of getting relief.

Q: Who is directing our attention to this goal?

A: Our bullies.

Hmmm. What if we, and not our bullies, directed where we put our attention? And what if, instead of focusing on finding relief from the discomfort of doubt, we chose to focus on our Greater Good goals?

Think again about Christof's admission that he was able to control Truman's life only because Truman allowed him to "direct" it. Now think about our own doubt bullies and the many ways they direct the reality shows that are our everyday lives, largely by focusing our attention on our worst doubts and fears. (What if *this* happened? What if *that* could happen?) Only by choosing to direct our own attention to bigger picture, Greater Good goals can we break out of Doubt.

"Whoa! Hang on, Bell," I hear you challenging. "Didn't you describe obsessions at their worst as all but impossible to get rid of?"

Yes. But I'm not talking about making them go away. I'm talking about choosing not to give them our attention. There's a big difference. We are not capable of choosing our thoughts; nor, for that matter, can we choose our feelings, per se. What we *can* do is choose how much *attention* we give certain thoughts and feelings. We can choose not to give our bullies' "what if" questions the power of our attention. This is tricky business, to be sure, especially because of the white bear phenomenon.

You're probably already familiar with this paradox — one frequently attributed to Tolstoy or Dostoevsky, and one that researchers have revisited in recent years — but if not, try this quick experiment: try *not* to think about a white bear at any point in the next five minutes. Not even once.

Can't do it, can you?

As any psychologist can tell you, the mere process of attempting to block out a particular thought assigns value to that thought, making it stand out from the multitude of other thoughts crossing your mind and hence making it more difficult to dismiss.

This, by the way, is one reason why advising someone stuck in Doubt to try not to think about the cause of his or her distress is generally the worst possible advice you can give. We with OCD get a lot of that advice from well-meaning friends and loved ones, many of whom also tend to suggest (with the best of intentions) that we who also battle depression just "cheer up" — another assignment beyond our control.

The process of directing our attention is something entirely different. It doesn't require us to avoid any particular thoughts or feelings. Instead it requires us to actively, willfully choose the targets of our attention. For me, this practice hinges on one key approach: acknowledging our thoughts and feelings with as much detachment as possible. If this sounds familiar, it's because I'm talking about the same mindfulness practice I discussed in connection with Step 3, though in this case we're using it to home in on constructive targets of our attention.

Bringing all this from the conceptual to the practical level, here's the most pragmatic, effective technique I have found for directing attention: picture your thoughts as passing clouds on a windy day. Start by imagining that you're lying on your back in a big grassy field, staring up at blue sky filled with all kinds of clouds, big and small. You watch these clouds float by, and as they move overhead, you allow yourself to state what you know about them. This big puffy one looks like a rabbit; it makes me feel happy. This round one looks like a cake; it makes me hungry. This dark and dense one looks like a prison; it makes me scared. And so on.

Now try making the clouds nothing more than placeholders for your thoughts. Instead of evaluating their sizes and shapes, simply acknowledge what each thought is and what emotions it evokes. *Here's a thought about my new job assignment; it makes me feel excited. Here's a thought about my daughter's great report card; it makes me feel proud. Here's a thought about last night's dinner; it makes me feel hungry. Here's a "what if" thought about harm I might have caused; it makes me feel extremely anxious.*

Aha! Here's the work of Director Doubt.

I acknowledge this thought, just like all the others. If I'm in a position to practice ERP techniques on it, I direct my full attention to it, knowing this is an opportunity to sit with the thought until the anxiety it provokes begins to subside. If I'm not in that position, then I choose to let it float by without trying to rid myself of the anxiety. If it stalls over my head, I acknowledge this.

Another thought, a mundane one about yard work I need to do, passes overhead. I acknowledge it. It floats by.

The "what if" thought reappears, as these thoughts do. I note this. I feel the anxiety and note this, too.

Soon, thoughts about my book project start passing overhead. These are the thoughts I need to focus on today. I willfully direct my attention to them.

The "what if" thought makes yet another taunting loop overhead. I acknowledge it, but again direct my attention back to the book thoughts. The anxiety from the doubt thought remains, but again I simply acknowledge it.

This is how attention directing works. It's not easy; it takes a lot of practice. But the better you get at kicking Director Doubt out of his director's chair, the more effective the process becomes for identifying fear-based doubts — without hiding from them or attempting to rid yourself of the anxiety they provoke — and clearing the way to direct your attention to your Greater Good goals and to act in empowering ways.

STEP 8. ACT FROM ABUNDANCE IN WAYS THAT EMPOWER

If you were to stop reading this book right here, I'm afraid the time (and, if you bought it, the money) you've invested in it would offer little return. Presumably you picked up the book because you're someone who struggles with uncertainty (although I guess I can't really be sure about that, now can I?). You're probably looking for help in developing your own road map for getting out of Doubt. By reading this far, you have done precisely what we've talked about in Steps 1 through 7 — choosing to recognize the potential of this book to help you pursue your own Greater Good goals and willfully giving these pages your attention.

But — and this is a big old *but* — you have not yet actually *applied* these strategies (unless, of course, you're a couple of steps ahead of me, literally), because this is what we're going to do now. *This*, as an old wrestling coach of mine used to say, is where the rubber meets the road. This is where we do the hard work. This is where we invest everything we have in the pursuit of our Greater Good.

When I look back on my own circuitous path to recovery — what I did right, what I did wrong — it's obvious now where I fell short for so many years: I did everything necessary to get better *except* the hard work. I went to my therapy sessions, I read all the books, I learned all about exposure/response-prevention, I went through all the right motions; but I only paid lip service to the process. Yes, I showed up at my therapist's office week after week, but I did the bare minimum necessary to convince her I was on board with her program; and, as I've already admitted, I all but lied to her about the homework I was doing in between visits. And then I got frustrated because I wasn't getting better!

If there's one thing I've learned from my recovery experience, it's that when it comes to escaping Doubt, there are no shortcuts. No way out of doing the hard work. No way around actually *acting*.

Accepting that we need to act, the question becomes, *How* should we act? The answer, I believe, is twofold: first, from abundance, and second, in ways that empower.

Acting from abundance is a popular concept in the success literature and one that makes a lot of sense to me. In essence, it means choosing to believe that there's enough to go around. Enough what? Enough everything. Period. The practice is often referred to as cultivating an "abundance mentality" — in contrast with what Stephen Covey calls a "scarcity mentality," in which one believes there is only a finite amount of everything. This distinction reminds me a lot of Einstein's purported question about whether or not the universe is friendly; and given that we've built this entire making-belief process on the premise that the universe *is* abundantly friendly, it makes sense that we choose to recognize the abundant nature of life itself.

This approach to acting is key because it's the antithesis of the way our doubt bullies would have us act. Think about how they use scarcity "logic" to lure us through trapdoors. *What if you lose your job (and can't find another)? What if your friends no longer like you (and there are no more friends to make in the world)? What if you try this project and fail (and you'll never have other opportunities)?*

Acting with abundance means affirming that — despite your bully's taunting to the contrary — you simply can't run out of those universal resources that move us toward our Greater Good. There will always be opportunities. You will always have your universal potential available to you.

The second key to acting effectively when stuck in Doubt is to question your motives and intentions at every turn. Are you doing this or that because it empowers you or others in some positive and constructive way, or because your bully wants you to? Put another way, are you acting out of purpose and service for a Greater Good, or are you acting out of fear and doubt to relieve your anxiety? If you learn to ask yourself this question regularly, you'll get very good at catching your doubt bully in the act.

This filtering process has proved to be invaluable for me in my struggles with doubt, especially in battling obsessions that involve possible harm to other people. For years I felt the need to report even the most ridiculous potential hazards to people in authority. Wobbly chairs at a restaurant? Tell the waiter! A splash of coffee on the floor of Starbucks? Report it to the manager! My bully would convince me that such reporting was the "good" thing to do because it was helpful to others. My therapist, however, would ask me to question that premise: "When you call over a waiter to tell him about a wobbly chair," she'd say, "are you *really* doing so to help him, or the next person who sits in the chair, or for that matter, anyone?"

"Uh, well . . . ," I'd stumble.

In reality, I was acting compulsively because my bully had posed the question *What if someone falls off this wobbly chair and gets hurt?* The question made me anxious. I hated this discomfort. I indulged my compulsive urge to report, and (temporarily) I felt better. My real motive here was to find relief. If I'd really wanted to act in an empowering way, I could have chosen not to do the compulsion, sat with the anxiety, and empowered myself with a demonstration of my ability to escape from Doubt.

One final thought on the process of acting. Sometimes we have to "act" to act. A longtime friend of mine has a favorite saying: "Fake it till you make it." It may sound like an ingenuous approach, but from my perspective it's a way of affirming my potential, even when I'm not feeling confident. As Marcus Bach quotes psychologist William James as saying, "When you don't feel the way you ought to act, if you just act the way you ought to feel, then you will feel the way you ought to act."

I grant you that this technique sounds a bit Pollyannaish. But I challenge you to give it a try. Invest in the concept. I think you'll be surprised. And if you're feeling really skeptical, well, *pretend* that you're not!

Fake it till you make it . . . all the way out of Doubt.

ON FREE WILL

Dan Millman

Q: In your experience, what have you found the role of volition to be in directing one's attention?

A: David K. Reynolds, PhD, the author of *Constructive Living*, provided me with the clearest approach to dealing with "what if" and all forms of doubt, uncertainty, anxiety, wondering, wishing, hoping, fearing. The key understanding is that in reality, we have little or no control (by our will) over arising thoughts or feelings. Therefore, we cannot be responsible for arising thoughts or emotions, since we are only responsible for that which we can control. As it turns out, the only thing we can control — and are responsible for — is our behavior, our actions. So the approach I recommend, as a "peaceful warrior in training," is to (1) accept our feelings and thoughts (positive or negative) as natural to us in that moment — to acknowledge that thought or feeling, and notice how it passes; then (2) focus on a constructive purpose, and (3) do whatever needs doing in line with our chosen purpose.

ON DIRECTING ATTENTION

Sylvia Boorstein

Q: One of the great breakthroughs in my own recovery was coming to understand that, while I can't rid myself of the nagging "what if" questions that plague me, I can choose not to give them my attention. Can you comment on this from your perspective?

continued ⇥

A: From the perspective of a meditator, when you begin to have confidence in the fact that it is possible to decide where you put your attention, then you are not held hostage by every random wind that pulls at your attention. And with that discovery, the trained mind has the capacity to say, I will change my focus of attention from the troubling thought that has captured it to what I am doing right now…or to my own body and thinking of ways that I can breathe deeply and truly. That I am in charge of where I put my attention gives me a tremendous taste of what I've found to be freedom. I've thought to myself, This is maybe part of what liberation means, not being held hostage. My whole body is subject to whatever might happen to it in this uncertain world, but my mind is free; I can put it where I want. I'm not saying that I, personally, can always put my mind where I want, but I think the hope of practice is more and more to be able to make the choice of where one puts one's attention.

ON PICTURING POSSIBILITY

Rev. Michael Moran

Q: Religious figures throughout the ages have talked about the concept of "picturing possibility." Can you give us an example?

A: In the New Testament, Jesus creates an image of a farmer who approaches a barren field. In order for him to have even the chance of a bountiful harvest, he faces months of backbreaking labor, and still no guarantee of success. It can be disheartening to see only the untilled, unplanted field

continued ⮑

stretching out before you, and the possibility of drought or flood, which could wipe out months of labor. But Jesus tells the man to open his eyes and lift up his vision and see that the field is already harvested. See it done before you even turn the first spadeful of soil, see the grain in full bloom, swaying in the wind, ready to be harvested. Focus on what you desire, not what you fear most. Seeing it done before there is any tangible evidence is a bold act of faith. It is a prayer of gratitude in advance of the desired outcome. Ralph Waldo Emerson echoed Jesus when he defined prayer as "contemplating the facts of life from the highest point of view."

Q: How about an example from your own life?

A: In 1999, I announced to over six hundred people that I intended to train for and complete a marathon before year's end. What was I thinking? I was over fifty, overweight, overworked, and totally out of shape. I invited others to join me in this spiritual and physical quest, and to my surprise over one hundred people signed on. I'm pretty certain that as they looked at me they thought, "Good Lord, if he thinks he can do it, I can at least try." At the first orientation meeting I told everyone not to focus on the daily grind but on the glorious day when we would all be crossing the finish line with huge smiles on our faces and with our hands in the air in joyous celebration. As a group, we prayed for the success of everyone on the team. Our collective investment was in the end result. We trained for over six months, and the one thing we promised ourselves and each other was that we would be there for each person when they crossed the finish line after 26.2 miles. It was that image, the prayers,

continued

and the promise that kept us training together on the long runs on the 90-degree days. Over fifty people finished as champions over their fears, doubts, and discomforts. It was a sight to behold as the last woman on our team crossed [the finish line], exhausted after being on the course for almost nine hours. She never took her eyes off the goal and the promise.

KEY POINTS

- Applying the principle of investment involves taking the following three steps:
    - ✳ **Step 6. Claim and exercise your freedom to choose.**
      Stephen Covey's proactive model reminds us that between stimulus and response lies our freedom to choose.
      "Exercising" your freedom to choose involves both
      - making use of this process as necessary, and
      - proactively using this process again and again to develop your skill in doing so.
    - ✳ **Step 7. Picture possibility and "direct" your attention.**
      As Covey suggests, the key to picturing possibility is to "begin with the end in mind."
      Directing your attention involves willfully choosing the targets of your attention.
      You cannot choose your thoughts and feelings, but you can choose the thoughts to which you direct your attention.
      Mindfully watching and labeling your thoughts and feelings allows you to acknowledge them in a detached, objective way, without assigning your attention to them.

* **Step 8. Act from abundance in ways that empower.**

  An "abundance mentality" affirms that there is plenty of everything to go around, consistent with the concept of a friendly universe.

  Questioning your motives for acting allows you to sort out when you are taking actions to empower yourself and others, and when you are taking actions because your doubt bully tells you to.

  Sometimes acting (as in taking action) involves acting (as in pretending), lending credence to the adage "Fake it till you make it."

> ## CHAPTER SEVEN
>
> # Surrender
>
> Fourth Principle of Making Belief

W e've all heard the battle cry "Never give up. Never surrender!"

If you'll allow me a bit of artistic license here, I'd like to suggest a modified mantra for those of us battling doubt: "Never give up. *Always* surrender."

Huh?

Well, first let me assure you I'm not attempting to play Yoda here with some deeply paradoxical advice. Despite their often interchangeable colloquial usage, *giving up* and *surrendering*, as I use them, are very different things. And although I spent a whole lot of years giving up again and again, only in recent years have I discovered the power of surrendering.

For me, *giving up* means admitting defeat, throwing in the towel, raising the white flag. In my battles with Director Doubt, it has meant saying, in so many words, "Do with me as you will." *Surrendering*, on the other hand, refers to the immensely powerful practice of accepting what I cannot control and letting go of my attachments to those things.

As I hope to show in this chapter, the difference between these two practices is enormous. Ultimately, it is the difference between remaining stuck in Doubt and taking the final, and most important, steps of making belief.

STEP 9: ACCEPT AND LET GO OF WHAT YOU CANNOT CONTROL

Years ago, while in the care of Dr. Y — the second of two trained psychologists who failed to recognize my OCD — she stared at me blankly and offered up this assessment: "You seem to have a very inflated sense of your own power." Since I had just described my concern about having been the cause of whatever horrific transgression had made a nearby driver lean on his horn earlier that day, I could understand, even then, where she was coming from. But in retrospect, I think what Dr. Y really meant to say was that I had an inflated sense of what's in my control. And on *that* point, she nailed it.

Like many people with OCD, I have battled what you might call hyperresponsibility issues for most of my adult life. Director Doubt loves to cast me as the villain in his movie scripts, and he is quick to suggest creative ways in which I might be responsible for one tragedy after another.

But as Dr. Y pointed out, I am not that powerful, at least when it comes to defining the extent of my control. And neither are you. In fact, I hate to be the one to break this news, but in the scope of an infinite universe, very little is in our control. Not the past, not the future. Not the weather, not our neighbors, not even our loved ones. Sure, we can take measures to affect all the above — except the past — but ultimately we are not in control. And here are two more items to add to our out-of-our-control list: our thoughts and our feelings.

Call this another "tough love" reality check, but . . . Carole, you are not in charge of your daughter's safety. Andy, you are not in charge of what your doctors know and don't know. Sarah, you are not in charge of whether or not your friends choose to like the new, sober you. Matt, you are not in charge of how comfortable or uncomfortable your surroundings make you feel. Terry, you are not in charge of what your colleagues think of you. *Jeff*, you *are in charge of everyone and everything*. (Hey, Director Doubt, out of here!)

Why are we so inclined to put ourselves in charge of things over which we have absolutely no control? I'm sure there are a whole host of psychological and philosophical explanations, but the one that stands out for me has my bully's fingerprints all over it. The more "problems" he can suggest are my responsibility to worry about (with my fear-based doubts), the more ways he has to suggest I "solve" these problems (by looking for trapdoors).

A hungry Octi wants to give me as many reasons as possible to feed him doubt-nuts. A conniving Director Doubt wants as many scripts as possible to keep me mired in Doubt and keep himself employed.

Recognizing what we're not in control of is a sobering, humbling process. Doing so, though, allows us to take the two leaps of faith that constitute Step 9: accepting and letting go of what we cannot control.

Acceptance, as I touched on in chapter 5, is a reconciling, if you will, between the way we'd like things to be and the way things actually are — *in that moment*. It does not mean throwing our hands up in the air and giving up all our universal power. On the contrary, it means exercising that power by using our free will to accept what's not ours to change so that we can direct our attention to that which is in our control.

In her book *It's Easier Than You Think*, Sylvia Boorstein paraphrases the Buddha's First Noble Truth in a way that rings true for me: pain is inevitable; suffering is optional. As she explains the Second Noble Truth: "Suffering is what happens when we struggle with whatever our life experience is rather than accepting and opening to our experience with wise and compassionate response."

Here's my own interpretation of this sage advice as it pertains to those of us stuck in Doubt: Uncertainty is inevitable (that is, out of our control); therefore, so too is the discomfort (pain) surrounding it. Suffering is what happens when we refuse to accept that uncertainty and the discomfort it brings (opting instead to chase trapdoors in a futile effort to rid ourselves of the discomfort). Therefore, the more we accept the sometimes painful discomfort of uncertainty, the less we actually suffer! Sounds a lot like ERP again, doesn't it? Funny how that keeps happening.

Let's say we're successful at recognizing that some particular outcome is not in our control, and we even manage to accept that reality. There's one more critical component of this process, and that's letting go of our attachment to that outcome. It's almost as if that particular outcome is a stolen diamond we clutch in our hands. We may recognize and accept that it's not ours to keep, but still we cling to it because of its value. At some point we need to let it go.

Because for me letting go implicitly involves a "recipient," for lack of a better term, I want to share with you a few thoughts on that matter, recognizing that the spiritual issues it raises are very personal ones that far exceed the scope of this book.

When I choose to let something go, I put it in the hands of the universe — again defined as that supportive cosmic system that helps me and all of its infinite parts pursue our highest and greatest good. Because my obsessing over outcomes beyond my influence is, in essence, attempting to wrest control from the universe, my surrendering that control is really returning it — or giving it back, if you will — to that very same universe.

This concept of responsibility transference has become a hot topic of OCD research, largely because there is growing evidence that the driving force behind obsessions is an excessive sense of responsibility for harm to oneself or others. Researchers are finding that these tormenting obsessions can often be curbed simply by transferring to another person that responsibility for harm.

This has certainly been my own experience. Time after time during my worst years, I would implore Sam to go through the house one final time before leaving for a vacation, just to be sure everything was in order. It's not that I thought she was better qualified than I to do this; my real motive was to transfer the responsibility for any calamity that might result from an oversight. In hindsight, this was also my motive in reporting wobbly chairs to restaurant owners and spilled coffee to Starbucks managers. Once reported, these issues were no longer my responsibility.

This behavior, of course, is itself a trap, and an especially counterproductive one. But psychiatrist Ian Osborn — an MD and recognized authority on OCD — has recently found a positive way to tap into this penchant of people with OCD to transfer responsibility, developing what he calls a "therapy of trust."

Osborn, along with a growing number of other professional therapists, has begun exploring the constructive role of religious faith in battling OCD, and his framework designates God, and not another person, as the recipient of the transferred responsibility. So, if an individual is obsessing over whether she might inadvertently infect a colleague with horrific germs, she surrenders her obsessions to God, accepting that He, and not she, is in control of this colleague's health.

This transference process entails a huge leap of faith, and Osborn's model next calls on OCD sufferers to prove that faith by willfully choosing not to perform the compulsions that they would otherwise feel compelled to do. The woman concerned about infecting her coworker, for example, would demonstrate her faith by forgoing her compulsion to scrub her hands again and again.

ON RESPONSIBILITY TRANSFERENCE

Ian Osborn, MD, author of
Can Christianity Cure Obsessive-Compulsive Disorder?

Q: Can you give us an example of your "therapy of trust" model?

A: Let's say someone is having trouble getting out of the house because they're obsessing that the furnace [and therefore their house] will blow up. That leads to uncertainty about whether or not they've checked enough. This is where we talk about transferring responsibility to God, putting the well-being of the house in God's hands. The key thing here is that we're not, in any way, getting a guarantee that the house won't blow up. We're not praying, "Don't let the house blow up." We're trusting God, with a certain degree of confident optimism, that he's not going to let that house blow up. Yet if, for his own reasons, God needs to let that happen, then we have to accept that. So it's a matter of transferring responsibility to God in this manner, not looking for factual certainty that the worst will not occur, but leaving the matter completely with the goodness of God who, in his providence, has power over all.

Q: And what's next from there?

A: The next step is to prove your trust in God by not doing your compulsion. A crucial point here is that putting trust in God is extremely pleasing to God. In treating your OCD, you grow much closer to God.

Q: It seems that this process still allows for the traditional ERP practice of sitting with one's uncertainty.

A: Right, because we're talking about transferring responsibility in a way that does not provide factual certainty. In fact, we can develop specific ERP exercises around this, designing ways to prove one's trust in God.

The beauty of this model, as I see it, is that it in no way skirts the need to accept and sit with the discomfort of uncertainty; in fact, for those with a belief in God, it suggests a powerful reason to sit with that discomfort, as an act of faith.

Because I have acknowledged the constructive role that religious faith can play in accepting uncertainty, I must also warn you about the trapdoors it can present, which in the extreme lead to a subset of OCD known as scrupulosity. People who battle this challenge often obsess about offending or displeasing God, and they develop compulsions ranging from elaborate, ritualistic prayers to excessive confessions. It's important to remember that doubt bullies respect no sacred boundaries, and that we must always be vigilant of the motives driving our religious practices.

ON SCRUPULOSITY

Alec Pollard, PhD, Director, Anxiety Disorders Center,
St. Louis Behavioral Medicine Institute

Q: Clinically speaking, what is meant by the term *scrupulosity*?

A: Scrupulosity is a form of OCD that involves religious or moral obsessions. Scrupulous individuals are excessively concerned that something they thought or did might be a sin or other violation of religious or moral doctrine. This type of OCD can be associated with mental or behavioral compulsions.

Q: What are some of the ways in which it manifests?

A: A scrupulosity sufferer might worry that having an immoral thought will result in eternal damnation, or that God's wrath will follow the imperfect performance of a religious ritual. Examples of mental compulsions include imagining sacred images, praying, and repeating passages from sacred scriptures

continued

119

in one's head. Behavioral compulsions might include excessive trips to confession, seeking reassurance from religious leaders, cleansing and purifying rituals, and acts of self-sacrifice.

Q: Religious or spiritual practices can be powerful sources of inner strength in battling doubt; yet in the hands of one's doubt bully, they can become distorted and misdirected. What advice can you offer for recognizing when this line has been crossed?

A: Unlike normal religious practice, scrupulous behavior usually exceeds or disregards religious law and may focus excessively on one comparatively trivial area of religious practice while largely ignoring other, more important areas. Far from being a source of strength, scrupulous rituals can be exhausting and make life more difficult .

Q: A recurring theme of this book is the importance of accepting uncertainty. I imagine this can be especially challenging for people battling scrupulosity?

A: It's true. The quest for certainty may be found in all forms of OCD, but it is particularly paradoxical in scrupulosity. Almost every major religion recognizes faith as a leap beyond fact and logic. In other words, faith is a commitment to something you cannot prove or know for certain. If you could prove it or know it for certain, it would no longer be faith. Scrupulous people are fruitlessly driven to be certain about their faith.

STEP 10. ALLOW FOR BIGGER PLANS
THAN YOUR OWN TO UNFOLD

So here we are at the edge of the Shadow, just one step shy of breaking out, one step away from the freedom we've been seeking. Are you ready to take this final step?

Before you answer, let's look back at the nine steps we've already taken. And if you'll indulge me, I'd like to recap *my* journey through these steps, mainly because I know my own footprints better than any others. By tracing them, I can suggest where these steps may or may not lead.

Let's rewind, then, to August 1997. I am deep inside the Shadow of Doubt, about as lost and entrenched as anyone can be in this cold, dark place. My bully, Director Doubt, is producing Oscar-winning horror films, casting me again and again as both the villain and victim. I am spending my days checking and washing, seeking reassurance, avoiding, protecting, and ruminating. Trapdoor after trapdoor lures me in. I am falling deeper and deeper.

And then, out of desperation, I make my Bargain with the Stars, as I've come to call my deal with the universe, at first demanding that it give me what I want before I return the favor, but then stumbling into the reality that things actually flow in the other direction. I commit to a Greater Good goal of doing something constructive with my story, going public with it in hopes that others might benefit and that I might give some meaning to all my lost years. In doing all this, I implicitly choose to see the universe as offering me the potential to achieve this goal. I have, in these early days, discovered the power of reverence, taking Steps 1, 2, and 3 in fairly rapid succession.

I begin my Crash Course in Believing and very soon find myself tested by a defiant Director Doubt, determined not to let me run him out of my life. Slowly, though, I develop my resolve, putting my commitment to my book project ahead of my comfort, again and again, and reminding myself of the Greater Good at stake. I take Steps 4 and 5 and survive my bully's best efforts to sabotage me.

I start to make real progress in my daily battles with Director Doubt and challenge myself to find opportunities to confront him head-on. With increasing detail I picture a life for myself outside Doubt, and I train myself to start directing my attention away from my bully's "what if" questions and toward my Greater Good goals. I come to trust that the resources I need are at my disposal. Day after day, I record my progress in my journal. Day after day, I keep walking out of the Shadow with Steps 6, 7, and 8.

As my project year passes, I become increasingly adept at the art of surrender, coming to recognize and accept just how much of what I *thought* I could control I really can't. I train myself to separate pain from suffering, reminding myself again and again that suffering is optional.

Everything is going just as (I) planned.

Before I know it, it's October 20, 1998. My index-card notations read "Day 365." My project year is over. My Crash Course in Believing is done. It's nearly midnight, and I am in my den, poring over my stacks of index cards, marveling over just how far I have come. I am clearly no longer entrenched in Doubt; I have found my way out.

But something is eating at me as I stare at my most recent "obsessions" and "compulsions" tracking cards. These cards are no longer crammed with items, as they were twelve months earlier. But neither are they *empty*, as I had pictured them. In all my planning, I have envisioned my success story ending with my conquering my OCD, in the sense of putting it behind me altogether. Clearly this is not to be the case.

I struggle with this issue over the next several months, as I begin stringing together my index cards to create a book manuscript. Maybe, I tell myself, I'm supposed to speak out as a "recovering" (and not a "recovered") OCD sufferer.

A year later, I have finished my manuscript. I am ready to publish it, ready to go public with my story. But I can't find an agent or publisher willing to take on the project. What's up with this? Where's the support of the universe when I need it? Maybe, I reluctantly tell myself, the timing is not yet right.

Another year passes, and another one after that, and yet another.

A very successful literary agent takes an interest in my story but tells me my manuscript is not yet ready. She offers me advice and resources and puts me back to work. What's up with this? Maybe, I tell myself, my own thoughts on how best to tell my story were not complete.

I spend another year rewriting and work with my agent to shop the book. Nothing. The rejection letters stack up, and so does my frustration. What's up with this? Where's the publisher to help me manifest my Greater Good? Maybe I just haven't found the right one to read my manuscript, I tell myself.

Soon it is 2003, and the unthinkable happens: I lose my job and, with it, my radio "platform." Gone is my greatest asset in the eyes of publishers. I don't understand how the universe could let this happen. I am devastated, but I refuse to let go of my plans to publish my book. I've invested far too much in my Greater Good goals, and I know in my gut that they're still mine to pursue.

Time marches on. Life's twists and turns lead me in directions I couldn't have imagined, taking me from a job I loved but lost in Sacramento to one in San Francisco that I had dreamed of holding ever since entering the business. Professionally and personally, things are good. Very good. I continue to hold the line in my battles with doubt, still motivated by the prospect of sharing my story.

And then, at long last, the offer comes in. I have a publishing deal. My book has a home.

On February 2, 2007 — nearly ten years after I'd committed to sharing my story, and nine since I'd thought I had everything in place to do so — *Rewind, Replay, Repeat* is published. My story is not the miraculous recovery narrative that I'd first envisioned; it is, I am told, much stronger, because it speaks to the ongoing challenge that is OCD. My book reads very differently from the first draft, which I'd thought said everything I wanted to say; it now conveys my message infinitely better. And my radio "platform" too looks very different from when I started my project; it has expanded in ways I couldn't have imagined.

My point in sharing all this is to explain, in the best way I can, just how Step 10 works. It demands of us that we allow room in our own best plans for even better ones. It requires us to tag the following words to our own affirmations, prayers, and goals: *This or something better!*

Doing this isn't easy. It's human nature to cling to our own plans. And for those of us who've had to wrest control of our lives away from doubt bullies, it can be even more challenging to surrender the things we might feel we now control. But this, I'm convinced, is how the universe works. It "sees" a larger, grander plan than you and I can see. It will support each of us in our individual Greater Good pursuits at every turn, but it will also fit these pursuits into what you might call a universal Greatest Good. In making belief, we each do our part to further that possibility.

Now then, are you ready to take that final step?

I want to close this section of the book with a couple of thoughts on the model of belief from which I've drawn my ten steps to making belief.

First, as I noted earlier, I have chosen not to discuss in depth the specific words that adorn the three sides (self, others, and life) of the cardboard pyramid that sits on my desk, deciding instead to focus on the model's four levels: reverence, resolve, investment, and surrender. I've also confined my discussion of the model to applications that pertain most directly to battling doubt bullies. Because of this, I want to point out a fundamental truth about pyramids: you cannot remove any one side and expect the other two to stand.

This truth is critical because it points to the holistic, interdependent nature of the principles of believing. Showing reverence for yourself but not others, for example, does not build the kind of belief we need to escape from Doubt. Nor does investing in the well-being of others without taking care of yourself. Your bully will likely try to convince you otherwise!

Finally, I want to point out what may already be obvious to you: making belief is an ongoing process. It's not something we do once and reap the benefits from forevermore. (If only it were!) I have found that I must apply the principles of reverence, resolve, investment, and surrender again and again and again; when I don't, Director Doubt is ready to take back control. The good news is that the more I work with these principles, the easier their application becomes. And when I fall short and find myself slipping back into the Shadow, I know my way out.

I hope this will always be true for you as well.

ON SURRENDER

Dan Millman

Q: What has your experience with martial arts taught you about resistance and surrender?

A: To most people, the word *surrender* means giving up, capitulating to someone else's power, view, or ego as a passive response to life. But from a higher understanding, surrender, or acceptance, is the most creative, assertive, constructive approach we can take to any moment. Because life is going to unfold as it will. We can ignore, deny, or resist, but these are ultimately not the most useful responses. The martial arts teach us to pull when pushed, or to push when pulled — to go with a force and shape it our way. We can take that same positive approach to whatever happens in life. This is not a new idea — it's turning lemons into lemonade. Or, as

continued ↵

Reinhold Niebuhr reminds us all in his Serenity Prayer, "God grant me the serenity to accept the things I cannot change, the courage to change the things I can, and the wisdom to know the difference. Living one day at a time, Enjoying one moment at a time, Accepting hardship as the pathway to peace..."

ON PAIN VS. SUFFERING

Sylvia Boorstein

Q: Coming to understand the distinction between pain and suffering has proved critical in my recovery, especially in terms of what I can and cannot control. Can you share a few thoughts here about this key distinction?

A: This is a very core and central point, Jeff. The Buddha would have said that pain in life is inevitable. Things happen, we lose the people we love, or they get sick, or we get sick, or something that we wanted very much to happen doesn't happen. Pain in life is inevitable. Suffering, he posited, was the extra tension in the mind that was unable to accept the truth of whatever it was that was happening. There are a lot of things in life that we can change. There are some things that we cannot change, and the narrative in the mind to have things other than the way they are, when they can't be, is what the Buddha said is suffering.

ON ACCEPTANCE AND SURRENDER

Rev. Michael Moran

Q: You lost your wife, Faith, in 2007, after one of the most courageous displays of surrender I have ever witnessed. Share with us, if you would, the lessons you have learned from this experience.

A: I had been noticing with increasing alarm that something was wrong with Faith, who was my partner in ministry for over twenty years. The once vivacious, totally organized, and spiritually focused person I had grown to adore and depend upon was struggling with even the most mundane daily tasks. She chalked it up to menopause, or fatigue from overwork, but on some level we both knew it was something else.

Daily she was becoming more forgetful and disoriented. I could see the fear and uncertainty beginning to show on her face as we both fought to keep our minds from going to the awful possibility that she could have a brain tumor, or worse. It's interesting how the mind wants to go to the worst-case scenario. Finally, I got up the courage to address this with her and she tearfully admitted something was radically wrong. We both cried and prayed as we considered our options. As ministers we had walked too many friends and families along the path of life-changing medical issues. This was different; this was my Faith.

Q: What did you find out about Faith's health challenges?

A: After months of inconclusive tests, the famous Mayo Clinic delivered the definitive diagnosis, a rare form of dementia which was incurable and totally untreatable. "I'm so sorry," her doctor said. The news was devastating. Our whole

continued ⮑

world changed in a matter of seconds. Gone was the life we had envisioned and looked forward to with eager anticipation. How could this happen to Faith, of all people? She was too young, too good, too healthy. She had overcome a horrific childhood and early adulthood to master many of her self-doubts and to lovingly minister to thousands of people of all faiths. It wasn't fair!

Q: What did you do after learning the diagnosis?

A: Our desire to find a cure for this "incurable" disease led to a whole host of alternative treatments. The cure kept eluding us, but the true healing began the day we truly surrendered.

Q: How did that happen?

A: Faith said, "Michael, it is what it is. The only question before us now is who do we choose to become now, as we walk this new path together?" That day we surrendered to whatever outcome was the highest and best for our souls' unfolding. We desperately wanted her to return to normal, but we surrendered to a cure or something better. With surrender came a sense of peace and nonattachment to a specific desired outcome.

So what could be better than a total cure? Well, it didn't look anything like we wanted it to look, but as the dementia claimed more and more of her, I grew to love and admire her even more, which I thought was impossible. I turned her daily care and sense of well-being into my primary spiritual practice. I prayed like I had never prayed before, but only for the strength to see her all the way through this. I decided to find or assign meaning to this

continued ⇴

"new normal." That decision enabled me to discover levels of love, faith, inner peace, compassion, patience, community, and strength that I didn't know were possible. She became my teacher of Big Love.

Surrender to a higher purpose released us from victimhood and brought meaning to her suffering and a deeper sense of connectedness and inner peace. Together we journeyed from awful to awe-full.

KEY POINTS

- In making belief, surrender does not imply giving up.
  - ＊ *Giving up* means throwing in the towel.
  - ＊ *Surrendering* means accepting those things we cannot control and letting go of our attachment to them.
- Applying the principle of surrender involves taking the following steps:
  - ＊ **Step 9. Accept and let go of what you cannot control.**
    Pain is inevitable; suffering is optional.
    In dealing with doubt, this means:
    - • The discomfort of uncertainty is unavoidable.
    - • Refusing to accept uncertainty causes great suffering.
  - ＊ **Step 10. Allow for bigger plans than your own to unfold.**
    In pursuing Greater Good goals, try to avoid becoming attached to specific details.
    Think, "This or something better!"
- Important reminders about making belief:
  - ＊ It takes all three sides (self, others, and life) of the pyramid model to keep it standing.

- Believing in others but not yourself (or vice versa), for example, will not lead you out of Doubt.
* Making belief is an ongoing process.
  - It's not enough to do it once!
  - Applying the principles of reverence, resolve, investment, and surrender becomes easier the more you do it.

PART THREE

CHOOSING GREATER GOOD

CHAPTER EIGHT

Better Than "Good"

The Greater Good Perspective Shift

On July 21, 2007, I found myself getting up to speak to a room packed with OCD sufferers and treatment providers. As I took the few steps from my chair to the lectern, I couldn't help thinking, *Well*, this *could be interesting*.

We were gathered, several hundred of us, in a Houston hotel ballroom, the site of the Fourteenth Annual OC Foundation Conference, and I was about to deliver one of the keynote speeches. The other two keynote speakers — also OCD "consumers," as we're known in mixed circles like this one — had both delivered powerful, uplifting accounts of their personal struggles and triumphs, very much in line with the theme of our talk: "Faith, Hope, and Inspiration."

My focus, I knew, would be a bit more provocative. I took a deep breath, thought *Here goes*, and launched into my talk.

For the next twenty minutes I proceeded to tell everyone in the audience what they were doing wrong. To my fellow OCD sufferers, I pointed out how fortunate we are to have a proven treatment strategy at our disposal, and that far too many of us are still looking for ways around it because we're unwilling to do the hard work. Ouch. To the treatment providers, I not so delicately suggested that all their brilliant work was essentially for naught if they couldn't keep their clients from dropping out — a major problem in OCD therapy. "If you're going to ask us to face down our worst fears," I challenged them, "then you'd better give us some dang good reasons to do so." Again, ouch.

I was proud of myself for sharing my thoughts so honestly, but I also accepted that this would likely be the last time I'd be asked to speak to this group.

Looking out over the crowd, though, I saw nodding heads and knowing looks. Everywhere. Perhaps, I thought, it was the OCD consumers agreeing with my assessment of what the professionals were doing wrong, and the professionals agreeing with my assessment of what the consumers were doing wrong. No matter. I was on a roll, feeling empowered with the zeal of a preacher at the pulpit on Sunday morning. Reverend Bell was ready next to offer his grand solution: motivation! *That*, I proclaimed, is what's missing in our OCD treatment model. We with OCD need to find it, and you who are treating us need to lead the way in that pursuit. More nods.

In my remaining few minutes, I offered a quick overview of what I would come to call my "Greater Good perspective shift" (GGPS) — a treatment motivation strategy that grew out of my own personal struggles and subsequent note-taking during my Crash Course in Believing.

Soon my time was up. I left the podium to more applause than I've ever received for a talk before or since. I had touched on something that resonated with a wide cross-section of OCD consumers and professionals, and their encouragement was just what I needed to move my outreach in this "tough love" direction.

In the couple of years since that talk in Houston, I have been privileged to present my GGPS concept to hundreds of OCD sufferers and treatment providers across the country. Through my outreach efforts, I've been able to share its principles at the grassroots level. I'm humbled by the way this GGPS approach has taken root in the OCD community, and nothing feeds my own Greater Good motivation more than trying to expand this concept's application in constructive ways.

To that end, I want to share with you a close-up look at this motivation strategy and its application in battling not only OCD but also the most basic of everyday fear-based doubts. I believe this perspective-shifting technique is the key to navigating the ten steps we've just covered, and therefore the key to breaking free of our doubt bullies. If the ten steps offer the pathway out of the Shadow, then think of the GGPS as a special GPS device (perhaps a *Greater Global Positioning System device?*) for keeping you on that path and away from the trapdoors.

My goal here is to provide you with not only an overview of the GGPS approach, but also examples of its use in the fear-based doubt situations our Shadow tour guides have offered. Ultimately, I hope you will be able to make use of the worksheet you'll find in this chapter to help motivate yourself to do the hard work of making belief.

THE GREATER GOOD PERSPECTIVE SHIFT

At its core, the GGPS is nothing more than a shifting of perspectives — from a decision framework based on fear and doubt to one based on purpose and service. This shift is willful by nature and therefore part of our decision-making process at every turn. It is, in fact, the impetus behind every step we've laid out as the means to making belief.

To make the shift, we need first to recognize the characteristics of both of the frameworks involved.

The Default Framework

I've come to refer to this first framework as a "default" one because it's how those of us who struggle with doubt normally frame most of our decision making, often without even realizing it. In this framework, our doubt bullies are in charge, presenting us with a black-and-white world and therefore black-and-white choices.

As our bullies present them, these choices are almost always framed as right versus wrong, or "good" versus "bad," based not on their inherent value but rather on the degree of anxiety they can leave us with. Our bullies would have us believe that, given two choices, the "good" choice is the one that appears to offer relief (if only temporarily) from our anxiety, and the "bad" choice is the one that requires us to sit with that anxiety. In this sense, it's easy to see how our bullies lure us to trapdoors — by default. Because deciding to check or seek reassurance, for example, seems to offer relief from our distress, our bullies convince us that these decisions are "good" ones to make. (Again, please note my consistent use of quotation marks around "good" and "bad" in this context; this is to stress that these labels are our bullies', not ours.)

Let's try a basic example and diagram what's going on through the decision tree worksheet in figure 8.1. (Yes, my inner Felix Unger *loves* these things!)

Say I am just arriving at a bookstore to give a talk about my new book. As I head into the store, my bully suggests that perhaps my hands aren't clean. *What if you're unknowingly carrying some horrific disease? What if you shake hands with a reader and infect him as well? What if that person becomes deathly ill?*

GREATER GOOD PERSPECTIVE SHIFT — WORKSHEET

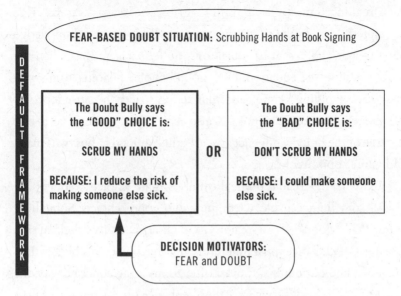

FEAR-BASED DOUBT SITUATION: Scrubbing Hands at Book Signing

DEFAULT FRAMEWORK

The Doubt Bully says
the "GOOD" CHOICE is:

SCRUB MY HANDS

BECAUSE: I reduce the risk of
making someone else sick.

OR

The Doubt Bully says
the "BAD" CHOICE is:

DON'T SCRUB MY HANDS

BECAUSE: I could make someone
else sick.

DECISION MOTIVATORS:
FEAR and DOUBT

Figure 8.1. Book Signing Challenge: Default Framework

Predictably, my bully suggests that I should scrub my hands thoroughly, because this will reduce the risk of my infecting anyone and therefore will reduce my anxiety. This is a "good" choice, my bully argues. The "bad" choice, my bully says, would be to give my talk and greet my audience without washing my hands and risk the possibility of making someone sick. Because I have done this dance with Director Doubt so many times before, the chances are pretty good that I'll find myself at the sink in the store bathroom before I even realize I have headed there. I have taken this first action by *default*. And now my bully wants me to scrub. As you can see from figure 8.1, if I remain in this default framework, fear and doubt will be my decision motivators, and they will lead me to make the "good" choice of scrubbing.

Now, let's put this example on hold, just long enough to consider a second and far more constructive way of framing my choices at this juncture.

The Greater Good Framework

Breaking out of a doubt bully's grip is never easy, and as I've attempted to show, the worst thing we can do is fail to acknowledge his presence and "what if" questions. So let's accept that when the bully is still in the equation, our "good" choice is going to involve taking (or avoiding) some particular action strictly because it promises the relief we're craving. Let's also accept that, because we're still not free of the bully's influence, we are still confined to but two (black and white) options.

But what if we can reframe the bully's "bad" choice as something else — something capable of trumping the "good" choice? Something better than "good" — a Greater Good choice? As I've defined it, a Greater Good choice must inherently involve objectives bigger than ourselves and our doubts. It must offer us, in some concrete way, the opportunity to be of service to others, enhance our own sense of purpose, or both. These objectives need not be grand or elaborate ones.

Service can be as simple as putting a smile on someone's face or making ourselves available to someone who needs us. It can involve giving of our time, talent, or treasure, in an infinite number of ways, always with the objective of empowering others in some constructive fashion.

Purpose is perhaps a bit more subtle, but it too can be very simple. Marianne Williamson once wrote, "The purpose of our lives is to give birth to the best which is within us." I think of this quote often when trying to identify for myself what actions I can take at any given moment that might enhance my own sense of purpose. What can I do to bring out the best in myself? To empower myself in constructive ways? The answers might include reading a book, getting some exercise, learning a new skill, undertaking a new challenge, or simply allowing myself to do nothing!

In identifying my own purpose and service goals, I often find it's helpful to remind myself of my core values. Interestingly, this practice is becoming increasingly popular in OCD treatment, thanks largely to the work of Steven Hayes and other ACT advocates, many of whom employ such techniques as eulogy writing as a means of helping their clients examine what's most important to them.

ON IDENTIFYING VALUES FOR TREATMENT MOTIVATION

Jeff Szymanski, PhD, Executive Director, OC Foundation

Q: **When working as an OCD therapist, you often recommended that your clients write their eulogies. Why?**

A: You write your eulogy to get in touch with the things that are most important to you — those things that you are willing to work hard for. That's one answer. Another answer is that because anxiety by its nature takes your attention and directs your attention, you need to be well in touch with your values and goals so that you keep the bigger picture open.

Q: **That can be tough for people with OCD?**

A: If you've had OCD from a very young age, all you've done is "manage," so you actually don't know who you are, you don't know what you like, you don't know what you don't like; you just know that you've been running from anxiety your whole life. People get to a point in treatment where they say, okay, now that the anxiety's starting to be reduced, I feel carved out. I feel empty. So when you ask, "What are your values?" and "What are your goals?" you hit a certain group of people who say, "I have no idea." I think the other thing that happens is that people say, "I've planned before, I've had goals before, the OCD has gotten so in my way, I

continued ➘

> feel like a failure, I don't want to get back out there again. It's too painful to hope. It's too painful to put this into words because I've always wanted it, I haven't gotten it, and I worry about whether I ever can get it; is the OCD really bigger than me?"
>
> **Q:** Why is it, do you think, that values assessment and other motivation techniques are proving to be so critical in treating OCD and other anxiety disorders?
>
> **A:** The work of dealing with negative emotions is extremely hard; you have to have in your mind a reason to do that hard work. If you go to the gym and you just focus on the fact that it is painful to do exercise, you're going to get off the treadmill. If you keep in mind that picture of the body you want to have, or the health that you want to have, that actually motivates you to do the hard work.

With this understanding of Greater Good goals, our next challenge is to reframe Director Doubt's "bad" choice as a Greater Good choice, identifying several purpose and/or service objectives that could be met by making this shift. This task is actually easier than it might seem.

Let's go back to the bookstore example. I am in the bathroom, at the sink. The water is running. My bully tells me my "good" choice is to scrub my hands until they're clean (as if that could ever happen). I am in the default framework.

What would all this look like if I could redefine my current situation within a Greater Good framework? Well, I'd still be at the sink. My bully would still be there taunting me with "what if" questions and making a case that scrubbing my hands would be the "good" thing to do. But instead of letting my bully's fear and doubt motivators lead me to the trapdoor of my protecting compulsion (in this case, scrubbing), I would choose to do the following:

1. Hit my imaginary "pause" button and realize that I can shift my decision-making framework.
2. Acknowledge the bully's presence and the "good" choice he wants me to make.
3. Reframe the bully's "bad" choice as a Greater Good choice by identifying several purpose and/or service objectives that could be met by making that choice.

In this example, my Greater Good choice is to go and give my talk without scrubbing. Working backward now, I need to identify for myself several ways in which making this choice is of service to others or enhances my own sense of purpose.

First, I remind myself that people are showing up at this store to hear me talk. I can be of service to them by getting out of the bathroom so I can give my presentation. I can also be of service to the manager by not keeping him waiting any longer; likewise for the guy behind me at the sink waiting for his turn!

Next, I remind myself how personally empowering these talks are for me. Giving them allows me to nourish my own sense of purpose, providing meaning to the many years lost to my disorder.

Finally, I remind myself of the ultimate sense of purpose I can find in standing up to my doubt bully: doing so allows me to get that much better at getting out, and staying out, of the Shadow.

Figure 8.2 depicts what this process looks like for me. It also points (literally) to the reason I am able to choose the Greater Good choice over the "good" choice at that moment —namely because, in this framework, purpose and service are my main motivators. It's just that simple.

Shifting Frameworks

A scientist once asked me what *proof* I had that this framework shift works. I responded, in so many words, "None," which I suppose is one of the perks of being outside the scientific community: I can get away with that honesty. I have no objective research or other statistical evidence to support the efficacy of what I've just laid out for you. None. But, as I explained to the scientist, what I do have in

GREATER GOOD PERSPECTIVE SHIFT — WORKSHEET

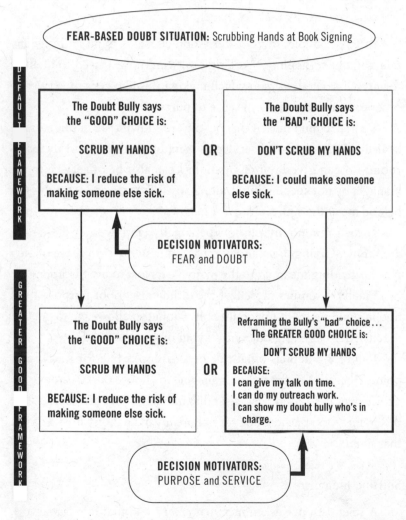

Figure 8.2. Book Signing Challenge: Shifting to Greater Good Framework

support of my methods is the most extensive case study I can get my hands on: my own. Everything I have shared with you — including the GGPS technique — has been field-tested repeatedly in the most challenging conditions, deep inside the Shadow of Doubt. In recent years, I've also had occasion to see numerous other people in my world benefit from the motivational framework I share in my outreach. But I draw no conclusions from their successes, only from my own.

I raise this here because at the very crux of my GGPS method is a working assumption I cannot prove: *given the opportunity*, purpose and service will trump fear and doubt as motivators every time. I have zero external proof of this. But time and again I have found it to be true in my own challenges. Even more, I believe that history itself bears out my contention better than anything. It seems to me that every real advance humankind has made has come when individuals or groups willfully chose to put purpose and service ahead of fear and doubt — in science, philosophy, geopolitics, and so many other pursuits.

Although I can't offer you any solid evidence of the power of choosing Greater Good, a growing number of scientists have begun looking for just that. At the University of California, Berkeley, for example, some of the nation's top minds are working together at the interdisciplinary Greater Good Science Center, researching the scientific aspects of such phenomena as compassion and altruism. Fifteen or twenty years ago, their research might have been written off as "out there." Today, though, their findings are popping up everywhere. (Look up "Greater Good Science Center" on the Internet and you'll see what I'm talking about.) The center's director, Dr. Dacher Keltner, recently published a book on this topic — *Born to Be Good* — and it thrills me to see how well it's selling.

ON GREATER GOOD MOTIVATION

Dacher Keltner, PhD, Director, Greater Good Science Center,
University of California, Berkeley

Q: How did you get interested in the science of Greater Good?

A: I got into it because of my frustration with basic emotion research, with its focus on doubt- and threat-based dimensions of human nature, and on "fight or flight" physiology and those elements of our brain and psyche. As an emotion researcher — inspired by Charles Darwin, who said that sympathy is our strongest instinct — I felt inspired to go after that and find it in our evolution and in our nervous system. And so our work is finding physiological underpinnings for service and compassion, how they guide really important moral notions — such as: I share a common humanity with other people for Greater Good — and how they are good for my own physical health and longevity. That's where we started and where we are.

Q: What are you finding in your work as to how Greater Good might be used to keep people doing treatment?

A: I think we are motivated in a couple of critical ways: one is to find a core principle that will be in your mind and be part of your life mission, providing a deep motive for some of the more day-to-day tasks you're living. There are studies showing that even if you work at a hospital cleaning bedpans, if you have a sense of a deeper motive, you're deeply satisfied. When people really realize that service and compassion are age-old and wise motives, it's a very powerful thing. And then the second thing is to link Greater Good principles to very practical ethics of everyday living. There

continued ⟿

are new studies coming out on social intelligence and emotional intelligence in the workplace and in couples and families showing those links. In the case of service, there's a whole set of behaviors that you can bring into your daily living that make life more meaningful — things like saying thank you and taking a moment to appreciate what you've been given, patting people on the back, or expressing appreciation to your romantic partner; these are really simple things that can have great utility.

Before leaving you with a couple more examples of the GGPS in action, I want to point out a critical caveat: when applying this approach, both choices you're evaluating must be feasible ones, by which I mean doable for *you*.

As I noted in Chapter 2, ERP is always approached on a hierarchical basis (that is, in a gradual and progressive way). When presenting patients with exposure challenges, therapists never ask them to act, or avoid acting, in any way that they are not yet ready for — and certainly never in any way that puts the patients or others in any kind of danger.

This point is crucial. If, for example, I found myself in a situation where my only two choices were to take a job as a taxi driver in San Francisco or remain unemployed, it might appear that my Greater Good choice would be to face down my remaining driving fears and take the job as a cabbie.

Sorry. Ain't going to happen! Not in this lifetime.

I take great pride in how far I've come in reclaiming my lost driving skills — skills I gave up because of my bully's constant taunting. Daily I ratchet up the degree of difficulty of my driving exposure challenges. Negotiating narrow streets, parallel parking, driving with passengers: I've added all of these back to my "doable" driving list.

But working as a taxi cab driver? That would be off the top of my hierarchy chart. And that's okay!

What's key here is that we need to approach decision-making challenges with practicality. That's why there is no substitute for working with a trained ERP therapist when our fear-based challenges begin interfering with everyday life — certainly when a diagnosis of OCD is made.

That said, let's revisit two of our tour guides back in the Shadow and see if we can help them use the GGPS to navigate clear of their trapdoors.

GGPS EXAMPLE: ANDY AND CHECKING

Remember Andy — my engineer friend who's been diagnosed with, and treated for, prostate cancer?

When we left him, Andy was entering the Shadow of Doubt, a place he's managed to stay clear of for most of his life. Since his diagnosis, Andy has been battling his doubt bully's taunts: *What if there's something out there that the doctors have overlooked?* Andy's bully wants him to scour the Internet for other possible treatments, just to be sure — to lure him to that trapdoor marked "Checking."

Let's fill in the blanks in Andy's GGPS worksheet (figure 8.3). First, let's identify the "good" choice. This one is pretty clear: Andy's bully wants him to spend hours online, researching prostate cancer and its treatment in case he finds information his doctors have missed.

The "bad" choice is simply to trust his doctors and shun any Internet research. To shift his decision-making framework, Andy must reframe his bully's "bad" choice as a Greater Good choice. To this end, he must identify the Greater Good served by his choosing to steer clear of Internet research.

For Andy, the real problem with his online checking is the toll it takes on his disposition. As he tells me, his greatest sense of purpose comes from the support role he plays at our radio station. As a long-time friend and coworker, I know exactly what he means. Andy, more than anyone else in our operation, is the person who makes the extra

GREATER GOOD PERSPECTIVE SHIFT — WORKSHEET

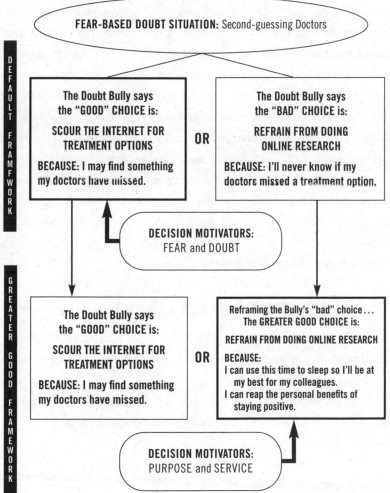

FEAR-BASED DOUBT SITUATION: Second-guessing Doctors

DEFAULT FRAMEWORK

The Doubt Bully says the "GOOD" CHOICE is:

SCOUR THE INTERNET FOR TREATMENT OPTIONS

BECAUSE: I may find something my doctors have missed.

OR

The Doubt Bully says the "BAD" CHOICE is:

REFRAIN FROM DOING ONLINE RESEARCH

BECAUSE: I'll never know if my doctors missed a treatment option.

DECISION MOTIVATORS: FEAR and DOUBT

GREATER GOOD FRAMEWORK

The Doubt Bully says the "GOOD" CHOICE is:

SCOUR THE INTERNET FOR TREATMENT OPTIONS

BECAUSE: I may find something my doctors have missed.

OR

Reframing the Bully's "bad" choice... The GREATER GOOD CHOICE is:

REFRAIN FROM DOING ONLINE RESEARCH

BECAUSE:
I can use this time to sleep so I'll be at my best for my colleagues.
I can reap the personal benefits of staying positive.

DECISION MOTIVATORS: PURPOSE and SERVICE

Figure 8.3. Andy and Checking

effort to brighten things up for all of us. Always quick with a smile and something positive (and usually clever) to say, Andy has a gift for making people feel good about themselves. It's uncanny.

Andy describes this role as his Greater Good. Because it nour-ishes him, personally, he sees it as a purpose motivator; but as I point out to him (from the perspective of a coworker), it is also a gift he offers others, so it is very much a service motivator as well. Either way, Andy has learned to remind himself of this Greater Good when he's tempted to spend yet more time at his computer in search of medical information. He knows that this (typically late-night) time is much better spent in bed sleeping, so he can show up at work the next morning with a smile on his face — and without bags under his eyes. He also knows how much better he feels about himself when he's not submerging his natural positive attitude in the desperation of his search; and he knows the difference that makes in his demeanor at work.

Armed with this motivation, Andy is able to shift his decision making from his default framework to a Greater Good framework and, in so doing, keep himself away from the checking trapdoor. As someone who benefits daily from Andy's gifts, I'm sure glad he's found a way to keep giving them!

GGPS EXAMPLE: SARAH AND PROTECTING

Sarah Allen Benton is a person who has worked hard to apply Greater Good goals in her life. Like me, she is on a quest to give meaning to many lost years.

In March 2009 Sarah went public with her story— an inspiring narrative of breaking free from addiction and of the lessons that she, as a high-functioning alcoholic, can offer others in similar situations. In my conversations with her, I'm always struck by how sincere she is about being of service to other people and how much personal inspiration she draws from the "gift" her challenges have given her.

As you'll recall, Sarah's problems with doubt began not when she was drinking, but rather when she stopped. Her bully was everywhere in her early days of sobriety, taunting her with "what if" questions about how she would navigate a life without booze. Because she'd been the life of the party for so many years, she grew more and more concerned about losing friends who didn't like the new, sober Sarah. At every turn, her bully reminded her that losing friends was quite possible, and encouraged her to "protect" her friendships by showing her friends that she could still hang out with them in bars. Doing so was torture for her in those early days, but she followed her bully blindly to this trapdoor.

Today, Sarah still has moments when she's tempted to put herself in situations she knows aren't good for her, simply because her bully suggests she should for the sake of friendship; but she also knows what's at stake, and she's learned to leverage her Greater Good goals to keep her bully at bay.

As depicted in figure 8.4, Sarah has learned to shift her critical decision making from the default to a Greater Good framework by reminding herself of the new service role she's carved out in her life and the motivation she draws from that role; so when the phone rings and she has to decide whether to put herself in a potentially triggering situation, she has a tool for picking the constructive option.

Sorry, Doubt; I'm afraid you're not going to hold back this inspiring woman from pursuing her Greater Good.

GGPS EXAMPLE: MANDI AND AVOIDING

In the two examples we just considered, the Greater Good motivators proved to be what you might call fairly grand. Andy draws inspiration from the magnanimous support role he plays at work; and Sarah, from her new life as an advocate for addiction treatment. I want to stress, though, that purpose and service motivators — especially in the moment — need not be sweeping ones; in fact, they can be extremely mundane.

Take the GGPS example Mandi recently shared with me. As I mentioned, my sister loathes medical TV shows because of the ammunition that they provide her doubt bully, who's always looking for ways to suggest that she or her family might be suffering from some obscure ailment or another that she hadn't considered.

The thing is, the rest of Mandi's family loves the show *Scrubs*; it's one of the very few programs they try not to miss. Recently she

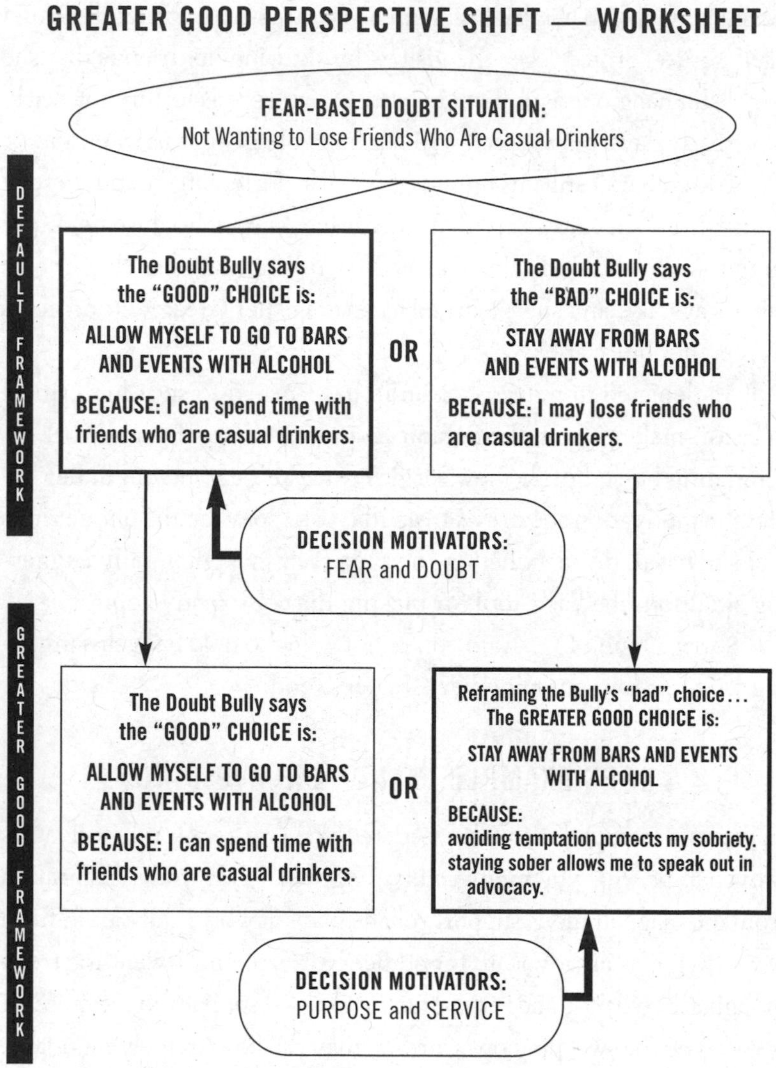

GREATER GOOD PERSPECTIVE SHIFT — WORKSHEET

FEAR-BASED DOUBT SITUATION:
Not Wanting to Lose Friends Who Are Casual Drinkers

DEFAULT FRAMEWORK

The Doubt Bully says
the "GOOD" CHOICE is:

**ALLOW MYSELF TO GO TO BARS
AND EVENTS WITH ALCOHOL**

BECAUSE: I can spend time with
friends who are casual drinkers.

OR

The Doubt Bully says
the "BAD" CHOICE is:

**STAY AWAY FROM BARS
AND EVENTS WITH ALCOHOL**

BECAUSE: I may lose friends who
are casual drinkers.

DECISION MOTIVATORS:
FEAR and DOUBT

GREATER GOOD FRAMEWORK

The Doubt Bully says
the "GOOD" CHOICE is:

**ALLOW MYSELF TO GO TO BARS
AND EVENTS WITH ALCOHOL**

BECAUSE: I can spend time with
friends who are casual drinkers.

OR

Reframing the Bully's "bad" choice...
The GREATER GOOD CHOICE is:

**STAY AWAY FROM BARS AND EVENTS
WITH ALCOHOL**

BECAUSE:
avoiding temptation protects my sobriety.
staying sober allows me to speak out in
advocacy.

DECISION MOTIVATORS:
PURPOSE and SERVICE

Figure 8.4. Sarah and Protecting

was enjoying watching TV with her family when an episode of *Scrubs* came on. By default she found herself about to get up and leave the room. But Mandi relishes her family time more than just about anyone else I know, and she reframed her decision in that moment.

As diagrammed in figure 8.5, Mandi acknowledged the compelling

GREATER GOOD PERSPECTIVE SHIFT — WORKSHEET

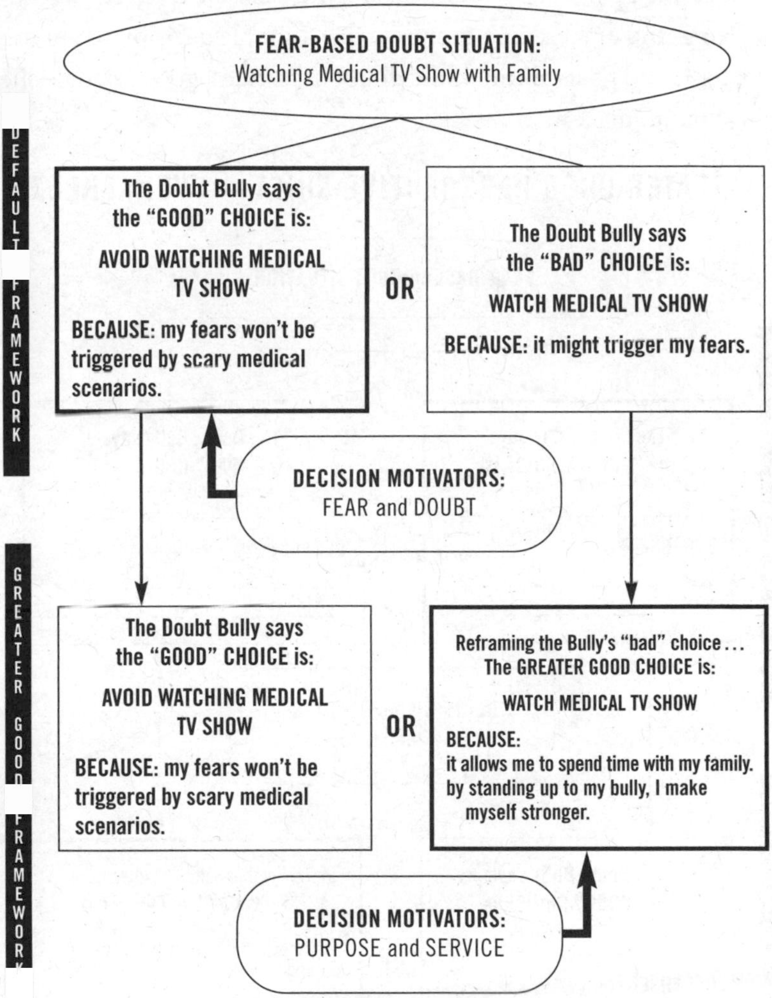

FEAR-BASED DOUBT SITUATION:
Watching Medical TV Show with Family

DEFAULT FRAMEWORK

The Doubt Bully says the "GOOD" CHOICE is:

AVOID WATCHING MEDICAL TV SHOW

BECAUSE: my fears won't be triggered by scary medical scenarios.

OR

The Doubt Bully says the "BAD" CHOICE is:

WATCH MEDICAL TV SHOW

BECAUSE: it might trigger my fears.

DECISION MOTIVATORS:
FEAR and DOUBT

GREATER GOOD FRAMEWORK

The Doubt Bully says the "GOOD" CHOICE is:

AVOID WATCHING MEDICAL TV SHOW

BECAUSE: my fears won't be triggered by scary medical scenarios.

OR

Reframing the Bully's "bad" choice...
The GREATER GOOD CHOICE is:

WATCH MEDICAL TV SHOW

BECAUSE:
it allows me to spend time with my family. by standing up to my bully, I make myself stronger.

DECISION MOTIVATORS:
PURPOSE and SERVICE

Figure 8.5. Mandi and Avoiding

case that her bully was making: that avoiding the show would be a "good" thing to do because it would allow her to avoid potential discomfort. But she chose to reframe the bully's "bad" choice (watching the show) as a Greater Good choice, telling herself that if she could sit through the show, she could be of service to her family (who certainly wanted her company) and she could enhance her own sense of purpose (by standing up to her bully and making herself that much stronger).

No grand or sweeping gestures. Just a simple decision to put her Greater Good goals ahead of the doubt-distorted "good" choice she was about to make.

GREATER GOOD PERSPECTIVE SHIFT — WORKSHEET

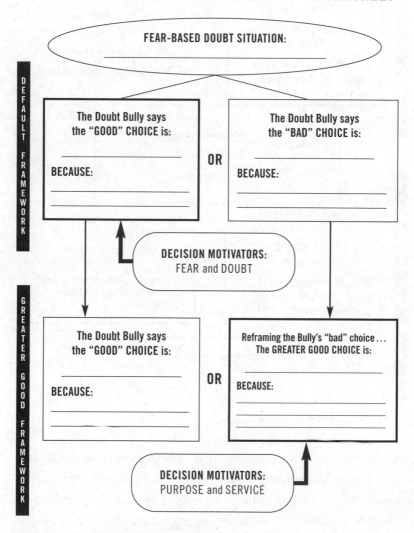

Figure 8.6. Blank GGPS Worksheet

YOUR TURN

I leave you here with a blank GGPS worksheet (figure 8.6) and a challenge: The next time you find yourself lured toward one of your bully's trapdoors, grab this worksheet and work your way through it. Identify your choices, as your bully defines them. Recognize, but don't buy into, the arguments he makes. Reframe the bully's "bad" choice as a Greater Good choice, spelling out with your purpose and service objectives why this is, indeed, the constructive choice to make. I think you'll be surprised by just how much power you have to make belief in the moment.

KEY POINTS

- The default framework:
    * Our doubt bullies are in charge and present us with black-and-white choices.
    * These default choices are typically framed as "right" versus "wrong" or "good" versus "bad," based not on their inherent value but rather on the degree of anxiety they can leave us with.
    * As our doubt bullies present them, "good" choices are those that appear to offer relief from our anxiety; "bad" choices are those that require us to sit with that anxiety.
    * Because compulsive actions such as reassurance-seeking, checking, avoiding, and ruminating reduce our anxiety (if only temporarily), they are almost always seen as "good" choices.
    * Within this default framework, decisions are based on two motivators: fear and doubt.

- The Greater Good framework:
    * While stuck in Doubt, our choices seemingly remain limited to two distinct options.
    * This framework acknowledges the perceived (though distorted) "good" of acting on compulsive urges to relieve anxiety.
    * This framework also introduces a Greater Good choice — one that in some way enhances our own sense of purpose and/or is of service to others.
    * Within this Greater Good framework, decisions are based on two motivators: purpose and service.
- Shifting frameworks:
    * Although when stuck in Doubt we are always left deciding between two distinct choices, we *are* capable of replacing one choice with another one.
    * In shifting from the default to the Greater Good framework, we can reframe a "bad" choice as a Greater Good choice.
    * This shift also replaces the default decision motivators of fear and doubt with the Greater Good decision motivators of purpose and service.
    * Because purpose and service tend to trump fear and doubt as human motivators, this framework shift enables us to make far more productive decisions.

CHAPTER NINE

Believers

Profiles of Belief in Action

Perhaps because of my lifelong struggles with doubt, I am increasingly fascinated by those rare individuals who seem to navigate uncertainty with ease and grace. We all know some of these people. They are the ones who remain unfazed by the changing circumstances of their lives, big and small. They mine their intellect-based doubt in the most constructive ways. They somehow stay calm and composed in the face of chaos. And they demonstrate, day after day, challenge after challenge, the very principles of belief that we've covered in these pages.

I've been privileged through my radio career and outreach work to have run across some extraordinary individuals who fit this bill: political leaders, athletes, scientists, celebrities, teachers, authors, entrepreneurs, philanthropists, and countless everyday folks who quietly choose to put their Greater Good goals above their doubts and fears. In this final chapter, I introduce you to five of these "believers": a former White House chief of staff (and current CIA director); a legendary screen actress and mental health advocate; a well-known financial analyst and broadcaster; a longtime, highly successful pediatrician; and a former Army Ranger and Rhodes scholar who led an infantry platoon in Afghanistan. Together, I believe, their stories offer a wealth of insight into this concept of making belief.

LEON PANETTA

I first ran across Leon Panetta more than twenty years ago, when he was a U.S. congressman representing California's Central Coast, and I was a cub reporter representing a (very) small radio station in San Luis Obispo. Representative Panetta impressed me back then as an especially grounded, sincere, and poised political figure; and in the many years since, my respect for him has only grown. That humble congressman from Monterey has gone on to serve as director of the U.S. Office of Management and Budget, White House chief of staff, and, most recently, director of the CIA. Along the way, he and his wife, Sylvia, founded the Panetta Institute, a nonpartisan center for the study of public policy.

Mr. Panetta and I spoke in December 2008, several weeks before he was nominated to serve as CIA director.

Q: **In the world of politics, can we assume that intellect-based doubt is a good thing?**

A: Anything dealing with human behavior is inherently uncertain; so when it comes to politics and governing, because it is such a human process, it is, without question, challenging in terms of the ability to get things done. I think if you approach these issues, understanding that there's no such thing as slam-dunking policy in a democracy, ultimately you have to analyze the problems, you have to try to figure out what the best solutions would be, and then you have to go about a process of developing support for the solutions that you think will work and try to figure out what the price is that you're going to have to pay in order to get people to come together and get things done. It is very much, obviously, an exercise that's based on intelligence, on capability, on preparation, on the ability to anticipate what the problems are. But I have to tell you, I think most of all, the only way you get through any of this is through sheer determination and grit. If you have the determination, if you're not diverted from what you're trying to get done because you may lose some votes, you may lose some opportunities, but if you never give up, then your chances of succeeding are a hell of a lot better.

Q: In the political world, how is it possible to determine when intellect-based doubt becomes fear-based doubt?

A: It's much easier to determine that in politics, because fear is the weapon that is always used by your opposition; they try to challenge whatever you're trying to do. Fear is a tool in politics, and I think the basic attitude is that if you can scare the hell out of somebody about what a possible solution may do to hurt them, then that works a lot better to stop things from moving forward than trying to base it on some sense of what someone is trying to accomplish. So, in politics, and I think probably in governing, everything to some extent begins based on kind of an intellectual approach to the problems that are there and how you try to solve them, but I think ultimately — because a lot of these problems are based in fear, particularly when the public is involved — ultimately the ability to deal with those problems depends an awful lot on whether you can confront that fear, and whether you can break through it by analyzing and understanding and recognizing that there either is or isn't a basis for the emotion that's attached to that fear.

Q: Have you found over the years that you sometimes need to do some gut checking — call yourself on letting your emotions get in the way of sound intellectual reasoning?

A: All the time. Because when you're confronting fear, it almost inherently [becomes] a backlashing fear, because you suddenly realize that you're not going to be able to deal with this intelligently, you're not going to be able to analyze it carefully, you are now dealing with emotion, and emotion is sometimes blind to the facts; and when that happens, you can sense it's happening, you can see it's happening, and the real challenge is, do you allow that fear to basically capture you and determine what happens, or do you try to still do the right thing? That happens in politics all the time.

Q: The two hallmarks for fear-based doubt, as I see them, are black-and-white reasoning and catastrophic thinking. In politics we see a lot of this, don't we?

A: There is no question that a lot of the gridlock we see in politics today, whether it's in Washington or Sacramento, is largely the result of black-and-white thinking in which, because both parties have been locked in partisan trench warfare, a lot of what they do is based on attacking the other side as being either irresponsible or incapable of really trying to solve problems; so it's almost always fear-based.

We see it in Sacramento right now [with] the whole fear-based approach [of] how do you deal with the state's [budget] deficit. I think intellectually everybody understands that if you're going to deal with that deficit you have to put everything on the table — spending as well as revenues — but when you try to do that, you're immediately confronted by the fear argument that if you try to raise revenues, you're nothing but somebody who's going to try to raise taxes on people who can't afford those taxes and you're simply somebody who's tax and spend; but on the other hand, [if] you're trying to cut spending, you're going to be attacked for hurting people, for hurting programs, for not caring about the individuals who benefit from those particular programs. So the attacks on both sides are basically fear-based, and the result is that...people then become fearful, and the representatives themselves then become fearful that they could lose their office by virtue of taking on these tough issues. Fear captures them, and they suddenly become incapable of solving the problem.

Q: **Is it safe to say that successful politicians have a tolerance for the discomfort of uncertainty?**

A: Oh, without question. I often used to say when I was chief of staff that my experience in the military served me a lot better than my experience in politics, because when you've got a mission to accomplish and you have a lot of incoming fire, it really serves you well to try to understand that that's going to happen, but you have to keep your eye on the mission, what you have to accomplish. That's really true. In every level in politics, from the presidency on down, you are [going to] confront constant uncertainty, you're going to confront situations that appear not only challenging but are going to surprise you, you're going to have to confront unpredictability almost all the time, and you've got to be able not to allow that uncertainty to overwhelm you; because if it does you're not worth much in terms of being a leader. So you really have to be able to adjust to what is almost a constant stream of uncertainty.

Q: **It seems to be human nature that we fall into traps of taking actions to try to counter the discomfort of uncertainty. What traps do politicians fall into? What counterproductive things do they do?**

A: The worst thing is that [this discomfort] paralyzes you and makes you incapable of stepping out and doing anything to deal with issues. You simply try to hide from those issues because they're either too controversial or sensitive, or they engender a lot of personal attacks on you. . . . And sometimes [politicians'] staff members will feed into that . . . for their own survival, sometimes encouraging [their bosses] not to take on what are controversial issues, or make controversial votes because it could jeopardize their political career. So it kind of feeds on itself and produces that kind of paralysis that makes leaders who are elected to deal with these issues incapable of doing so.

Q: Is it possible for political leaders to become paralyzed by fear-based indecision?

A: I think what you described can happen, because you're in a situation where you're going to get conflicting advice as to what you should do. [For example,] when we were about to send troops into Haiti, there were a lot of people around the president's desk — secretary of state, chairman of the Joint Chiefs of Staff, various military commanders, secretary of defense — all basically, at that point in time, trying to give advice as to whether or not the troops ought to go in. . . . Ultimately, it's the president who has to make that decision knowing full well all of the risks involved, but I think the president, at some point, has to be comfortable with himself in knowing that if he does nothing, if he doesn't take that step, that worse consequences will happen. Even though what he is about to do is risky, even though it may involve lives, ultimately that risk is worth taking because the alternative is simply not acceptable.

An [example] I can remember is when the Mexican peso

was collapsing. It was pretty clear that if we didn't take any action to support Mexico, not only would their economy fall apart, but it was likely [our inaction] would also impact our trade and our economic relationship with Mexico. Well, supporting Mexico financially was not popular; all the polls showed that it was not something the American people wanted to do. The Congress didn't want to do it. The leadership in the Congress was unable to get any votes to support it, so the president had to face a decision. He had all this opposition — the opposition of the American people, the opposition of the Congress, and the opposition of the leadership; and yet, at the same time, his economic advisers were saying, If you don't do this, it's going to produce even worse consequences. So the president had to face the decision of saying, I'm going to go ahead and do this; I know what the risks are, I know I'm probably going to incur a lot of anger from the American people for doing this, but in the end, I think it's the right thing to do for the country. And I think in many ways throughout history, it's those presidents who ultimately make those decisions based on what they think is in the best interest of the country — despite the fear, despite the risk, despite all of the arguments against what they are doing — that ultimately succeed.

Q: **Is it safe to say that these examples represent putting the Greater Good above twisted distortions?**

A: I guess we could all debate what the Greater Good is; in the end, it really is in . . . that leader's mind that the Greater Good is being served. I think if the individual bases it on that — that it really is better to take this action, it really is in the interest of the country, as he sees it — then I think . . . chances are that it's more likely to be the right decision.

PATTY DUKE

In May 2008, I had the opportunity to go out to dinner with Anna Patty Duke Pearce and her husband, Mike. The two were in San Francisco for a gala marking the sixtieth anniversary of the Mental Health Association of San Francisco. Anna was to be the keynote speaker and I the emcee. The prospect of sitting down with an Oscar-winning icon of the entertainment world was thrilling, and the reporter in me couldn't wait to talk with her about her life as a movie star. I couldn't have imagined how much more meaningful our actual conversation would turn out to be. That night over dinner, and the following night at the gala, I got to know not Patty Duke, the film and TV legend, but Anna Pearce, the courageous woman who went public with a story of battling mental illness long before it was acceptable for public figures to do so. We talked not as a reporter and a celebrity, but as two people whose lives had been touched by biochemical brain disorders. Funny what a great equalizer mental illness can be.

I've asked Anna to share some thoughts about making belief here, both because of the unique circumstances of her incredibly public and challenging life and because of her inspiring commitment to put her Greater Good outreach efforts ahead of her own acting career. Although it's hard to imagine anyone not being familiar with her work, here are the highlights:

Anna was born in New York in 1946. She first appeared on TV as a contestant on *The $64,000 Question* at the age of twelve. At sixteen, she became the (then) youngest person ever to win an Academy Award in a competitive category, taking home the Oscar for her portrayal of Helen Keller in *The Miracle Worker*. From 1963 to 1966, Anna starred in her own TV series, *The Patty Duke Show*, in which she played not one but two lead characters. She went on to have a successful pop singing career and win three Emmy awards. Along the way, she battled a series of mental health challenges, which she now knows were related to bipolar disorder. In 1987, Anna published *Call*

Me Anna: The Autobiography of Patty Duke, in which she divulged her mental illness, a subject she tackled again in her follow-up book, *A Brilliant Madness: Living with Manic-Depressive Illness*. In the many years since, she has become a role model for countless mental health advocates, including me, and has touched millions of lives.

Q: **I want to start with your decision to go public with your story. You did so at a time when very few public figures were talking about issues as delicate as mental illness.**

A: That's right. The advice that I received from agents and lawyers and some friends was "Don't do this. If you want to have a career, don't do this." And, of course, that struck home.... It wasn't so much the career I was worried about, it was making the money for my children and me. And yet ... there was something indescribable inside of me that said, You've got to do this, you've just got to do this. There was fear of being ostracized. There was fear, again, that I was losing employment. And yet, whatever it is, the thing [that] is inside of me, it insisted [on my] informing the public — I kind of thought of myself as a scientist; I didn't have the right to keep this information under cover.

Q: **Talk, if you would, about some of the "what if" questions your doubt bully posed to you.**

A: Once I began speaking out, traveling the country, talking to a variety of groups in the mental health world and outside the mental health world, almost always, before I would give my talk, there was a [voice of doubt] that said, You don't know what you're talking about, mind your own business, sit down and shut up. And then someone would be introducing me and the old show horse had to go on. Even while giving my talks to this day, my doubt bully will show up, *during* the talk — that kind of sabotage that we do so well to ourselves. And yet [something in me] insist[s] I plow on.

Q: As you know, I've come to refer to my own doubt bully as Director Doubt. In reading your books, I can't help thinking that you must have felt that much of your life was being "directed."

A: Oh my dear. My life was controlled, down to what time I went to the bathroom. And I'm not kidding about that. And the devastating thing back then was that I was not only being controlled about my acting — what parts I should play and what parts I shouldn't — I was being controlled in my entire being, including my soul. It has taken many years to sort of patchwork my soul back together.

Q: As you came to direct your own life, in what ways has that empowered you?

A: As I thought I was all grown up and ready to start my own life, the ghosts and gaps of the past became enormous, and what I did was fulfill the prophecy of the people who raised me — the prophecy being that without them, I am nothing. And I withdrew, withdrew actually from myself, and in an ass-backwards way, finally being diagnosed with bipolar has been freeing. It gave me a hook to hang my doubts on and to finally be aware of them and be able to, not look at all of them right away, but over time systematically peel the onion.

Q: If you'll indulge me with this example, I'd like to explore how the concept of Greater Good has factored into your career. Let's say you're taking on a new movie role. I can imagine your doubt bully saying, "Don't do it . . . what if you fail?"

A: Hey, get out of my brain!

Q: And I'm guessing this bully says you should avoid the role . . . in case you get bad reviews.

A: That's right; if I just stand still, I can't make any mistakes. And of course what I do when I stand still is make the mistake of covering my psyche and my confidence. This [debate] happens every time there is a job.

Q: So, if your bully tells you it would be "good" to avoid new roles . . . what's the Greater Good that motivates you?

A: The Greater Good is finding what it takes to put one foot in front of the other. I'm about to do a play that I can't talk about yet, and I know very well that I will be fully prepared, that I will have all the insight I need. Still, I also "know" as I take my first step on the stage that I am going to create a disaster. But . . . as I take the next step, there's no disaster — usually — and if there is a disaster, in my terms (whether I forget a line or don't walk to the right place on the stage), nobody dies from it. Sure, I will have some recriminations when I get into bed that night, but they pass. Over and over again, I'm learning the lesson is [to take] action.

Q: It seems the entertainment business is inherently uncertain — with actors living one project at a time.

A: Yes, we are gypsies, we are transients, and what better place for someone who is basically unbalanced to flock to?

Q: What have you learned from dealing with all that uncertainty?

A: I don't know if it's the blessing of age — I know all the curses of age — but the blessing of age allows me to accept — to see the demon for what it is, and either look to remove it or find a creative way to go around it.

Q: I have to ask you, Anna, about your unique film connection to Helen Keller. It's hard to think of anyone who had to live with more life uncertainty than Helen Keller.

A: It is wonderful that you made that connection, because there really is a connection, a lifelong connection for me. I was intimately involved — playing Helen Keller (in the first *Miracle Worker* movie) and, years later, playing her teacher (in the second *Miracle Worker* movie). What an example, what a map for me to follow. And I didn't always follow it consciously. I think that the emotional connection, as a child, with that kind of spirit has been incorporated in me. It may well be, and I never thought of this before, but it may well be one of the aspects that allowed me or forced me to go public.

TOM SULLIVAN

Whether you know it or not, chances are pretty good that you've seen or heard Tom Sullivan share his financial insights. With a daily TV program on the FOX Business Network and a three-hour radio show beaming across America, it's hard to miss Tom on the commercial airwaves. As countless fans will tell you, this is a good thing.

Tom and I spent eight years working together at KFBK Radio in Sacramento, and throughout that time he impressed me with his pragmatic, commonsense approach to personal investing. Over and over again, I heard Tom warn his listeners about the perils of letting their emotions get in the way of their judgment — advice he put to work for many, many clients through his former private investment practice. Working on this book, I found myself thinking about that advice and Tom's seeming unflappability when it comes to the inherent uncertainty surrounding investing. I wanted to know what lessons he felt the investment world had to offer the rest of us when it comes to sorting out our healthy and unhealthy doubts. What I didn't realize until he connected the dots for me in our interview was just what critical roles *each* of these forms of doubt plays in the give-and-take of a free market.

Very enlightening — and sobering — as I think you'll agree.

Q: Given that risk is inherent in the financial world — and therefore so too is uncertainty — do most successful investors have a high tolerance for that discomfort?

A: Yes, it's mandatory. To be a successful investor, you must be willing to accept risk. People like Ted Turner and Virgin Airlines' Richard Branson have taken enormous risks that have paid off. We haven't heard about other people who have taken enormous risks because they failed. Risk turbocharges the rewards but also turbocharges the failures.

Q: In working with clients, did you find that some people do better dealing with uncertainty than others?

A: Yes, and I've had to take people out of the stock market because they would call and say, "I couldn't sleep last night I was so worried about my stock portfolio. I'm looking at _____" and they would fill in the blank: the markets, the interest rates, the election — whatever it might be. They couldn't sleep at night. And I would say, "There's no investment worth losing your sleep or your health over."

Q: **You talk often about the roles of two emotions — fear and greed — in driving investment decisions. Can you explain?**

A: There is something called the sentiment index, and it literally measures pessimism and optimism: the more pessimistic the index gets, the more the indications are, historically, that we're close to a [market] bottom. When optimism is off the charts, we're close to the top. Investing is nothing more than going back and forth between fear and greed. People hear me say that, and they think that greed is bad. But I say, no, not necessarily: you want to achieve your promotion because you'll have more income. That is healthy greed. But then there is also unhealthy fear about things.

Q: **And the investment world plays off this?**

A: When the markets are in trouble and people are fearful, the banks will run ads in the newspaper that say, "We're the biggest. We're the strongest. We're the oldest." When the markets are sailing and doing wonderful, the same banks will run ads saying "We pay the most. We pay the highest. We pay the best." And so they play off of your fear and your greed.

Q: **Don't we also see this phenomenon in market trading?**

A: The stock market is simply an emotional auction house. That's all it is. There's a buyer and seller for every stock, for every transaction. So when you see those billions of shares traded every day, there's a buyer and seller on both sides of those. [The buyer's] emotions suggest that things are near the bottom, things are going to get better, things are going to go higher — optimistic emotions. And the [seller] is fearful that things are going to go lower. So you have two emotions playing off each other, and there you get the market. It really is an emotional auction house between fear and greed and optimism and pessimism.

Q: That fear you talk about breeds uncertainty. How do you, personally, sit with that?

A: I don't open my 401(k) statement when the market's down; I don't look at it. I know it's down; I just don't want to look at it. It's not because I'm sticking my head in the sand. It's simply that I avoid taking in too many negatives. I rely on my strength, and I rely on history. I know this has happened before, and it will happen again. It will turn.

Q: Given the current market and all the uncertainty surrounding it, what is your advice for people who find themselves moving into fear-based doubt?

A: Well, always remember [investing] is a game we play against each other, and I'm assuming there will be other people that will drive prices down because of their concern and their fear. I'm assuming that they'll drive prices down to such a point that I can take advantage of their fear, and I will step in and buy. I'll be on the buy side of their sell. As I said, it is an emotional auction house.

Q: So, in the investment world, you can make the case that those who use their intellect-based doubt actually benefit from those who fall into fear-based doubt?

A: Yes. Let's say I have a brand-new Chevrolet and I'm worried about General Motors. I say to you, "Jeff, I just bought this car last week for $25,000, but I'll sell it you for $20,000." Maybe you're not interested, but what if I later call you up and say, "I'll sell you my brand new car for a buck," would you do it?

Q: Sure.

A: So it's not a question of if, it's a question of price. At some point you will say, "Gee, Tom, I'm sorry you're so fearful about your nice brand-new Chevrolet, but for that price, yes, I'll take it off your hands."

Q: It sounds pretty harsh — even recognizing that all the players are there voluntarily — but the financial world is largely a battle between intellect-based and fear-based doubts, isn't it?

A: Yes. If you're able to keep your wits about you — or, as you've described it, if you're able to keep your fears intellectual — you will be able to benefit from somebody else's emotional fear.

LEWIS T. NERENBERG, MD

Unlike Leon Panetta, Patty Duke, and Tom Sullivan, Lew Nerenberg is not a familiar name. Prior to publishing *Rewind, Replay, Repeat*, I had never heard of him. But in getting to know him over the past two years, I have come to greatly admire his unique take on living with uncertainty, and I wouldn't be surprised if someday his name too becomes a well-known one.

Dr. Nerenberg is a very successful pediatrician in Northern California. He also has a family member with OCD, so he's all too familiar with the power of doubt bullies and the devastating toll they can take on lives. Perhaps because of his exposure to the OCD world, Dr. Nerenberg has developed what strikes me as especially keen insight into the uncertainty inherent in the practice of medicine.

Dr. Nerenberg's medical experience spans four decades and includes work in both emergency medicine and general pediatrics. He has also done extensive work in bioethics and physician-patient communications, and he has taken a personal interest in the issue of physicians' mistakes and their aftermath.

We first met when Dr. Nerenberg reached out to me with an interest in my Greater Good approach to dealing with OCD, and, as I think you'll see, he employs a very similar approach to his own work in medicine:

Q: Let's start with the role of intellect-based doubt in the medical world. It certainly would seem it's a key ingredient.

A: Well, I think that as I've gone through [my career], I've become impressed that it's more important to be attentive and caring than it is to be brilliant. And part of caring involves thoroughness. That means constantly questioning that no stone has been left unturned.

Q: At what point does intellect-based doubt cross over into fear-based doubt?

A: I think the last perceived mistake we've made, the last person who got sick on our watch because we weren't quite thorough or smart enough, in our mind, can affect the way we practice for the next month, or year, or couple of years.

Q: Can you give us an example?

A: Let's say a young child comes in with chronic abdominal pain. He's squirrelly, and he's happily running around the room. Then I feel his belly, and I'm sure he has nothing serious. I've seen this a million times; I can figure it out in seconds. But three days later I find out he's in the hospital and has been diagnosed with a tumor filling up his whole belly. It's so big that I didn't feel it, and other people didn't feel it either. So just as I'm getting comfortable with my intuition and experience, along comes a left hook that I never would have dreamed of, and that affects my practice pattern: maybe now I have some emotional doubts the next time it comes around.

Q: How might this impact your practice?

A: If this delay of diagnosis had made a difference — it didn't in this case, but let's say it did — I might be inclined to start ordering more X-rays and CAT scans.

Q: And that's bad?

A: Clearly the risk and burden of excessive radiation is greater than the risk of disease for the majority of those kids.

Q: So, in ordering these extra tests, your driving motivator would be alleviation of your own discomfort?

A: That's right. There are many terms for this, including "treating yourself, not the patient." Some of it is out of selfishness, but some of it is out of fear, and some of it is out of guilt and shame — the prospect that you would be exposed before the world for screwing up — somebody died or somebody was harmed because you weren't thorough enough, or smart enough, or caring enough, and you'd be shamed.

Q: It's interesting: your line of work puts a premium on checking, doesn't it?

A: Yes. We check values, we check lab tests, we check in with people with phone calls, we check that a specimen actually got to the laboratory. We check and we recheck. Checking is built in.

Q: Can this go too far?

A: I suppose that if you stayed late and you had just double-checked all your tests and you started wondering, *Did I really do all those?*, that could take away from your balance, your ability to take care of yourself, your ability to be involved with your family, and ultimately to take care of your other patients.

Q: Do you see that?

A: It's hard to say, because it's just so much of the job. So much of the job is checking. There's a great stigma against being someone who doesn't check.

Q: Perhaps I missed my calling! How about reassurance-seeking? Do doctors fall into this trap?

A: Sure, when they're younger, by and large, but also when they're doing something that's new to their scope of practice. The saying in medicine is "See one, do one, teach one." You watch someone do a lumbar puncture, and next time you do it, and the third time you teach someone else [how to do it]. Some people are paralyzed by this, but I think it's usually when they're younger. If they need that much reassurance as time goes by, they're just not in the right area.

Q: I'd imagine doctors must sometimes find themselves ruminating about their decisions, especially ones that prove to be mistakes.

A: Yes, but at a certain point, you realize it's time to move on. If you practice long enough, you are going to make mistakes, and somebody is going to be affected. That's part of your job description, and it's no excuse not to go to work on Monday. Some of this has to do with acceptance and surrender. You [as a doctor] are not God; you didn't make all those people who got well get well, and you didn't make all those people who got sick get sick. You made mistakes that Mother Nature forgave and a few that Mother Nature didn't, and that's part of the job. You can't be cavalier about it, but you need to keep working.

Q: Let's talk about avoidance. Are there times when physicians' self-doubt would have them avoid procedures?

A: Yes. Some emergency-room doctors will set a fracture, and others will call in an orthopedic surgeon; some will intubate a patient, others will call in an anesthesiologist. Maybe some are more gun-shy. Avoiding something you're not trained for is one thing, but if you're avoiding something just because it scares you, it impacts that patient and how soon he or she gets treatment, it impacts how long your other patients wait for you, it impacts your colleagues, it impacts the overall cost of health care to society. This is avoidance. In the extreme, I've seen people stop practicing medicine altogether because it's terrifying.

Q: Allow me, if you would, to use that scenario as an example of the Greater Good motivation built into practicing medicine. If a doctor's doubt bully says, "Get out of medicine because it's terrifying," what's the Greater Good response?

A: Well, it certainly has to do with service. I have a job where I get to look into people's eyes and I feel like I am of genuine service. It's nourishing to help others.

Q: Let's return to the kid with the stomachache for a moment. If, in the wake of your delayed diagnosis in that case, your doubt bully convinced you that ordering lots of extra tests would be "good," what would be a Greater Good that could trump that urge?

A: Well, I suppose you'd have to step back for a second and ask, What's the goal here? If I focus on my patients' well-being, then I'll end up with peace of mind. The higher purpose at that moment is caring for my patients.

Q: If I'm hearing you correctly, you wouldn't necessarily be of service to them if you were ordering tests that could be counterproductive.

A: That's right; before I order or do a test I have to ask, *Am I doing this because I'm caring for them, or because I'm scared and I want to take care of myself first?* If I step back and ask this, and if the purpose is that I'll be caring for my patients, then I, too, will be taken care of.

CRAIG MULLANEY

Craig Mullaney first appeared on my radar when an assignment editor at work forwarded me a news release about his new book, *The Unforgiving Minute: A Soldier's Education*. We thought it might be interesting to talk to Craig about the emerging shape of the all-voluntary military in the wake of 9/11. I arranged a phone interview and, through it, learned about a remarkable thirty-year-old man who had graduated second in his class at West Point, completed Ranger school, attended Oxford as a Rhodes scholar, led an infantry platoon in combat in Afghanistan, taught history at the Naval Academy, and served as chief of staff for then-President-elect Obama's Pentagon transition team.

I wrote and produced my stories for the station and moved on to my next assignment. But, as I did, I couldn't help thinking how enlightening it would be to ask Craig about how he'd dealt with, and thrived in the midst of, all the uncertainty inherent in his military career. This was an area we hadn't explored at all in our phone chat. With only days left before my editing deadline, I asked my editor for permission to wedge one final interview into this chapter, and I sent Craig a note asking if he was open to the idea. He graciously agreed to sit down with me during a brief trip to San Francisco several days later.

I suspect that the "supportive universe" I write about might very well have had something to do with the crossing of our paths; as I think you'll see, this interview sums up better than I ever could the messages I hope to convey in this book.

Q: **This is a book about living with uncertainty. What has your military training and experience taught you about dealing with uncertainty in a healthy way?**

A: To fundamentally accept that the world you inhabit as a military officer is filled with uncertainty and ambiguity and that you as an individual can't control all the variables that impact danger or your risk, and to find a way to use your intellect to discern the best path forward through that fog of war.

Q: **I would imagine that in military situations, healthy doubt serves you well.**

A: Healthy doubt, particularly about your environment, is very important. When you're on patrol in what could be a hostile village or a nonhostile village, for example, you don't really know which it is: it depends on what happens during that patrol. Your obligation in that situation as a leader is to anticipate threats and risks and dangers and to always be thinking of ways that you can mitigate those risks and dangers. And that's sort of a healthy doubt, what we would call a healthy paranoia — that a good officer plans for the worst and hopes for the best, rather than the other way around.

Q: Give us an example of when healthy doubt can become unhealthy doubt.

A: That can happen when, despite your best efforts to mitigate risk, something bad happens. A vehicle hits a roadside bomb or someone gets shot in an ambush. That pierces your veil of invulnerability, and it can be very difficult to go back out again over that same terrain facing what now seems like a more certain probability of danger than before. It's not an abstraction; it's real, and you're confronted with your own mortality.

Q: What might your doubt bully say in that situation?

A: Don't go back on patrol. Don't leave the gate. Find an excuse not to take your platoon back out over the same ground. Maybe you can just avoid that altogether if you find some alternative mission.

Q: I can imagine someone like you has had to face a doubt bully at every step of your military career. What were the bully's taunts as you headed off to West Point?

A: What if I have to come back home after a week and face my family and friends with my head hung in failure? What if I screw up when I'm taking my first physical fitness test and I just wash out? What if I don't get along with my roommates, whom I'm stuck with for the six weeks of basic training? What if I get the meanest SOB ever as my squad leader/platoon sergeant, who's got it in for me? What if people make fun of my Rhode Island accent? Those kind of things.

Q: How about your first combat assignment?

A: What if I don't bring all of my men home? I sat down and wrote letters to their parents and their spouses saying that I'd do everything in my power to keep their husband or their son safe. That's a lot of weight to bear at twenty-five years old and with guys from eighteen to thirty-four that are my responsibility.

Q: I would think that ruminating could become a trapdoor for military leaders.

A: Yes, certainly after a traumatic event. You may not be doing it intentionally, but things will replay in your head, and certain images or sounds will act as triggers for this memory loop. And sometimes it's like this film reel that just keeps playing over and over again. I can recall, after one of my soldiers was killed in our first firefight, replaying my actions in my head over and over again, and looking for places where I might have made mistakes, and second-guessing myself. I became angry and frustrated at the things I couldn't remember and couldn't see out of this film reel.

Q: At some point did that become counterproductive?

A: It's certainly counterproductive, because you need to glean the lessons from the operation — whether it's a training exercise or a combat operation — and incorporate that in your training as you move forward; but you've got to move forward. There's another mission that's going to be different, and you've got to concentrate on that. You can't afford to have 20 percent of your brain thinking about what happened yesterday.

Q: I want to talk next about the concept of choosing Greater Good. I define this as pursuing goals based on purpose and service. What do these concepts look like in your world?

A: The military attracts people who want to become stronger, faster, or of better character. As an institution, you're always afforded ways of measuring your progress against these goals — this sort of self-improvement. I want to be a better athlete. I want to improve my leadership skills. I'd like to be a better leader. Get better grades. The military gives you no shortage of purposes to which to apply yourself. This is the classic Army credo: "Be all you can be." It was very effective, because I think it struck a nerve in a lot of people — seeking to be better people and to have a purpose to their life. And that's sort of service to others; it's essential to the experience. It's hard to separate the two. All of the training is designed to make you realize that the team is stronger than the individual; that you can accomplish much more in concert with others; and that, some would say, you have an obligation as a citizen to help protect or defend your country — especially during a time of war. It's a distinct privilege to serve in uniform.

Q: **One of the themes of this book is learning to sit with the discomfort of anxiety and seeing that it dissipates on its own. How important is this in the military?**

A: It's very important. It was a revelation to me, in reflecting on my experiences, that there was only so much that I could do to influence the shape of a battle. The adversary and the environment have votes in the outcome. You can do everything right and people will still get hurt or killed, and it doesn't all fall on my shoulders as a leader to prevent that. Ultimately, I couldn't keep my men safe. It was sort of a naive understanding to equate mission performance with safety. Mission performance is to accomplish the mission and to accept a certain degree of risk, yet mitigating that risk through training and planning. The only way to keep my men safe would be to never go on a patrol. I had a lot of anxiety about the consequences of the decisions I'd made as a platoon leader for years afterward, thinking back to this firefight on a ridge where one of my men was killed.

Writing about it and then sharing that with family and friends and talking about it on the road, at bookstores, and on radio and television . . . is an exposure to the anxiety that eventually makes it less powerful.

Q: **What you've just described sounds a lot like exposure therapy — confronting fear-based doubt head on.**

A: I've always tried to do that. What's the only institution in the country I could go to where a bookworm couldn't survive? It was West Point; I'd have to confront that. The only course I struggled with in high school was history, so when I went to West Point, I decided to become a history major. I was afraid of heights, so I joined the skydiving team.

Q: **I'd like to revisit your experience in which your platoon was ambushed on patrol and your mission is to go back on patrol over that same ground. Remind us of what your doubt bully says is the "good" choice.**

A: The doubt bully probably says the "good" choice is to pick a different area to patrol, or don't go on patrol at all, or let the platoon sergeant or squad leader go out on patrol, or don't take the whole platoon out.

Q: **And your "bad" choice would be . . . ?**

A: The "bad" choice, I guess, is to go on patrol.

Q: **So if you're in that situation and this voice of doubt is telling you to avoid, what do you identify as Greater Good to motivate yourself?**

A: The Greater Good is to say I have a duty as a commissioned officer in the Army, and I have an obligation to my men to lead by example, and to lead from the front, and to confront my fears and to lead with that resolve. To go on the mission and perform to the best of our ability, recognizing that there are certain things that we won't be able to control, and that something bad might happen again, *but* that you have to endure what you can't avoid, and embrace it, and remember that the road home leads through this valley of fear and doubt.

Afterword

raud.

My doubt bully loves this epithet and fires it at me as a weapon of last resort, a final, poison-tipped arrow in its quiver, with the power to take me down. Usually, this happens on the heels of some significant triumph in my life; so it's no surprise, really, that I'm feeling its toxic sting as I write these words, much as I felt it a decade ago when scribbling down the final journal entry of my Crash Course in Believing.

Back then, Director Doubt was quick to point out that, despite my best efforts to rid myself of OCD, I had not. Three hundred sixty-five days after I'd set out to wrest my life back from the grip of doubt, obsessions and compulsions were still a part of my life — a significantly smaller part of my life, yes, but still a part of it. Who was I to go public with what would inevitably be positioned as a success story?

A fraud, that's who, my bully was quick to answer.

Today, the dialogue is all too similar. I've come to understand over the years that my OCD successes are less about ridding myself of the disorder than they are about learning to effectively manage it, so Director Doubt's taunting on this front has lost much of its power. Still, like any good bully, mine has found a new front on which to attack.

So, you're an expert now on the principles of making belief?
An expert? No, I respond to my imaginary nemesis. I'd call myself more of a "student" of them, really.
Haven't you filled this book with "specific strategies for making belief"?
Yes, but —
Can you honestly say you, yourself, have mastered these strategies?
No, but —
What about this notion of choosing Greater Good? Do you do this consistently?
Well, not always, but —
Fraud!

This is how my new dialogue with Director Doubt goes, and I share it with you for two reasons: first, because it serves as a reminder of just how hard our bullies will work to sabotage our successes — especially when those triumphs threaten their very existence; and second, because it points to the need for yardsticks that we (not our bullies) can use to measure our progress in making belief.

I have three such yardsticks I use for myself. They stem from the very principles of belief and Greater Good that we've explored in these pages, and, for me, they represent the outward results of living in accordance with them:

- Passion for life
- Kindness to others
- Grace of self

Every morning I say these words out loud, adding to them the following line: "May these, and only these, be the yardsticks with which I measure my triumphs this day." Hours later, before I climb into bed, I take a few minutes to review my day and answer three (leading) questions for myself:

- In what ways did I demonstrate passion for life today?
- In what ways did I demonstrate kindness to others today?
- In what ways did I demonstrate grace of self today?

The answers are sometimes disappointingly short. They often make me want to focus instead on my many shortcomings that day. But the beauty of these particular yardsticks is that they have built into them an element of surrender, one that requires me to leave behind all that doesn't serve my Greater Good. I can't, for example, demonstrate grace while beating myself up over my shortcomings. Nor can I live with passion while consumed by mistakes of the past. In my experience, these yardsticks encourage me to find at least some examples of how I've demonstrated my belief on any given day, and I use these triumphs to remind myself of what I am capable of. I also use them to motivate myself the next day through the next set of challenges awaiting me.

Measured by Director Doubt's characteristically black-and-white metrics, I suppose I am a fraud. I have indeed failed to master many of the principles about which I've written. But the reality is, I'm a work in progress. And so are you. Life is a classroom with very gray walls. We are students — learning, growing, triumphing, and, yes, falling short again and again. I want to reiterate this here because I believe your greatest challenge moving forward will be the same as mine: remembering what we already know — that, thanks to free will, we, not our doubt bullies, are in charge of the decisions we make and therefore in charge of our lives. Yes, our bullies can taunt us in seemingly endless ways. No, we can't make them disappear from our lives. But we can always —always — *choose* to exercise our free will. Always *choose* to pursue Greater Good goals. Always *choose*, again and again, to *make belief*.

And when we do, our bullies don't stand a chance.

Here's to believing . . . beyond our doubts!

A NOTE FROM JEFF BELL: Throughout this book, I have written about the power of pursuing Greater Good goals. My own such goals have led me to donate my time to the International OCD Foundation (formerly the Obsessive Compulsive Foundation), in hopes of playing a small role in raising awareness about this disorder. I have also decided to donate a portion of this book's proceeds to the International OCD Foundation, and I'd like to encourage you to help me raise funds for this nonprofit group and the important research and education efforts that it supports. If you are able to make a donation, please consider doing so by visiting the organization's website at www.ocfoundation.org. In any case, I hope you'll help spread the word about this book and, in so doing, help spread the word about the power of choosing Greater Good.

The Ten Steps Out
When Stuck in Doubt

- Reverence
    1. Choose to see the universe as friendly.
    2. Embrace the possibility in every moment.
    3. Affirm your universal potential.
- Resolve
    4. Put your commitments ahead of your comfort.
    5. Keep sight of the big picture and the Greater Good.
- Investment
    6. Claim and exercise your freedom to choose.
    7. Picture possibility and "direct" your attention.
    8. Act from abundance in ways that empower.
- Surrender
    9. Accept and let go of what you cannot control.
    10. Allow for bigger plans than your own to unfold.

Acknowledgments

Writing this book has proved to be very much like assembling a jigsaw puzzle, and had I spread out all the pieces in front of me early on I'm sure I never would have attempted to put them together. Fortunately, I wasn't that organized. (Apparently, my inner Felix Unger was on vacation when I first set out on this quest.) All I initially knew was that I wanted to write a book about confronting uncertainty, and I wanted to include a wide mix of perspectives beyond my own. I certainly never imagined that the mix would grow to include nearly thirty contributors spanning more than a dozen fields, or that I would spend countless hours collecting their thoughts and stories. Luckily for me, I was working with a team of professionals who did the literary equivalent of holding up the puzzle box and pointing to where all the pieces should go.

I am greatly indebted to the following members of this team: my agent, Susan Schulman, who believed in the potential of my outreach long before I, myself, knew what it would look like; Georgia Hughes, who invited me to join the New World Library (NWL) family and has treated me with the warmth and kindness of a family member at every turn; Erika Büky and Kristen Cashman, whose keen eyes and insights have strengthened every page of this book; NWL's Munro

Magruder and Kim Corbin, and Teak Media's Jackie Herskovitz, whose creativity and dedication are helping take my message far and wide; and Mandi Friedel, whose uncanny ability to complete my sentences before I even start them has, once again, proved invaluable. I can't imagine tackling a book project without you, Mops.

In addition to writing the foreword to this book, Dr. Michael Jenike served as my scientific advisor and provided immeasurable support. I am extremely grateful for his contributions and, even more, for his friendship.

Dan Millman, Sylvia Boorstein, and Michael Moran each gave of their time so that I might share in this book the invaluable wisdom that I, myself, gleaned from their teachings on my journey. Thank you.

Drs. David Burns, Tamar Chansky, Steven Hayes, Jennifer Hecht, Stephen Hinshaw, Dacher Keltner, Ian Osborn, Alec Pollard, Jeffrey Schwartz, and Jeff Szymanski loaned me their expertise and, in so doing, allowed me to include insights far greater than my own. Thank you all.

Andy Ellis, Carole Johnson, Jared Kant, Mandi Friedel, Matt Solomon, Sarah Allen Benton, and "Amy," "Lisa," and "Terry" opened up their lives to me so that I might capture many key lessons learned through their courageous journeys. Please know how very grateful I am.

I am humbled to be in a position to thank the five remarkable individuals whose interviews make up the final chapter of this book. Thank you, Leon Panetta, Anna Patty Duke Pearce, Tom Sullivan, Dr. Lew Nerenberg, and Craig Mullaney for so graciously giving of your time. Your accomplishments and your abilities to *make belief* inspire me greatly.

I would love nothing more than to list each of the many friends, relatives, and colleagues who have supported me in so many ways since going public with my story. Unfortunately, that's not possible.

Instead, I will call out a much shorter list of individuals whose support proved critical in creating this book: John Christgau, Tammy Daily, Belinda Lyons, Wayne Manning, Ivy Ridderbusch, Lisa Spinali, my many talented colleagues at KCBS, and, of course, Mom and Dad and Uncle Mikey. I also owe a special thanks to Joy and Dick Innes for opening their home and their hearts to me during so much of the writing process.

I am blessed, indeed, to be working alongside so many gifted and passionate individuals on the OCD Foundation board of directors. My sincere thanks go to Diane Davey, Joy Kant, and the rest of the board and staff for supporting me in my outreach.

As always, my deepest gratitude of all goes to my JGs: Samantha, Nicole, Brianna (and Zaxi). You are my best friends and greatest teachers, and I love you forever.

Notes

Each note corresponds to the page number listed in the left-hand column.

CHAPTER 1. *WITH* OR *WITHIN* DOUBT?

5   *Historian Jennifer Michael Hecht does a masterful job*: Jennifer Michael Hecht, *Doubt: A History* (New York: HarperOne, 2003).

13   *So, as bestselling author David Burns likes to point out*: David D. Burns, *When Panic Attacks: The New, Drug-Free Anxiety Therapy That Can Change Your Life* (New York: Broadway Books, 2006).

CHAPTER 2. OCTOPUSES CHEWING DOUBT-NUTS

18   *Studies suggest it takes people with OCD an average of fourteen to seventeen years*: Obsessive Compulsive Foundation, *What You Need to Know about Obsessive Compulsive Disorder*, www.ocfoundation.org.

20   *My favorite description of this cycle*: Edna B. Foa, PhD, and Reid Wilson, PhD, *Stop Obsessing: How to Overcome Your Obsessions and Compulsions* (New York: Bantam, 2001) and Tamar E. Chansky, PhD, *Freeing Your Child from Obsessive-Compulsive Disorder: A Powerful, Practical Program for Parents of Children and Adolescents* (New York: Crown, 2000).

CHAPTER 3. TRAPDOORS

39   *As Jared details in his inspiring memoir*: Jared Kant, *The Thought That Counts: A Firsthand Account of One Teenager's Experience with Obsessive-Compulsive Disorder* (New York: Oxford University Press, 2008).

49   *As she recounts with great candor in her courageous new book*: Sarah Allen Benton, *Understanding the High-Functioning Alcoholic: Professional Views and Personal Insights* (Westport, CT: Praeger, 2009).

CHAPTER 4. REVERENCE

67   *"It requires an act of faith, a volitional act ...":* Marcus Bach, *The Will to Believe* (Los Angeles: Science of Mind Publications, 1973), 101.

68   *Dan Millman, whose remarkable personal story*: Dan Millman, *Way of the Peaceful Warrior: A Basically True Story* (Boston: Houghton Mifflin, 1980).

70   *The three tenets of his logotherapy philosophy*: Viktor Frankl Institute of Logotherapy, *Main Tenets of Logotherapy,* www.viktor franklinstitute.org.

70   *"What man actually needs is not a tensionless state ...":* Viktor Frankl, *Man's Search for Meaning* (Boston: Beacon Press, 1959; reprint, 1992), 110.

72   *"Mindfulness doesn't erase confusion ...":* Sylvia Boorstein, *Happiness is an Inside Job: Practicing for a Joyful Life* (New York: Ballantine Books, 2007), 106.

72   *Brain scientist Dr. Jeffrey Schwartz and science writer Sharon Begley tackle these issues*: Jeffrey M. Schwartz, MD, and Sharon Begley, *The Mind and the Brain: Neuroplasticity and the Power of Mental Force* (New York: HarperCollins, 2002).

CHAPTER 5. RESOLVE

80   *"The central question . . . is not how we avoid uncertainty and fear ...":* Pema Chödrön, *Comfortable with Uncertainty: 108 Teachings* (Boston: Shambhala, 2002), 7.

85 *a five-and-a-quarter-inch "Obsessive Compulsive Action Figure":*
   The Obsessive Compulsive Action Figure is sold by Archie
   McPhee & Co., www.mcphee.com/items/11561.html (accessed
   July 30, 2009).

87 *Out of curiosity, I began looking into ACT*: Steven C. Hayes, PhD,
   *Get Out of Your Mind and Into Your Life: The New Acceptance and
   Commitment Therapy* (Oakland, CA: New Harbinger, 2005).

CHAPTER 6. INVESTMENT

96 *The one that has had the most profound impact on my life*: Stephen
   R. Covey, *The Seven Habits of Highly Effective People: Restoring the
   Character Ethic* (New York: Simon & Schuster, 1989).

100 *"Look where you are going..."*: Emmet Fox, *Find and Use Your Inner
   Power*, in *The Emmet Fox Treasury: Five Spiritual Classics* (New
   York: HarperCollins, 1992), 121.

101 *You're probably already familiar with this paradox*: Daniel M.
   Wegner, *White Bears and Other Unwanted Thoughts: Suppression,
   Obsession, and the Psychology of Mental Control* (New York:
   Viking, 1989).

106 *"When you don't feel the way you ought to act..."*: Marcus Bach,
   The Will to Believe (Los Angeles: Science of Mind Publications,
   1973), 35.

CHAPTER 7. SURRENDER

116 *"Suffering is what happens when we struggle with whatever our life experience is..."*: Boorstein, *It's Easier Than You Think: The Buddhist
   Way to Happiness* (New York: HarperCollins, 1997), 19.

117 *Researchers are finding that these tormenting obsessions*: C. Lopatka and
   S. Rachman, "Perceived Responsibility and Compulsive Checking:
   An Experimental Analysis," *Behaviour Research and Therapy* 33
   (1995): 673–684.

117 *Therapy of trust*: Ian Osborn, MD, *Can Christianity Cure
   Obsessive-Compulsive Disorder? A Psychiatrist Explores the Role
   of Faith in Treatment* (Grand Rapids, MI: Brazos Press, 2008).

CHAPTER 8. BETTER THAN "GOOD"

138 *"The purpose of our lives is to give birth to the best . . ."*: Marianne Williamson, *A Return to Love: Reflections on the Principles of A Course in Miracles* (New York: HarperCollins, 1992), 65.

143 *The center's director, Dr. Dacher Keltner, recently published a book on this topic*: Dacher Keltner, PhD, *Born to Be Good: The Science of a Meaningful Life* (New York: Norton, 2009).

CHAPTER 9. BELIEVERS

162 *In 1987, Anna published*: Patty Duke, *Call Me Anna: The Autobiography of Patty Duke* (New York: Bantam, 1987) and *A Brilliant Madness: Living with Manic-Depressive Illness* (New York: Bantam, 1992).

173 *His new book, "The Unforgiving Minute"*: Craig M. Mullaney, *The Unforgiving Minute: A Soldier's Education* (New York: Penguin Group, 2009).

Index

Page numbers in *italic type* refer to figures.

G

H

About the Author

Jeff Bell is a longtime veteran of radio and television news and currently coanchors the afternoon news at KCBS Radio in San Francisco. His first book, *Rewind, Replay, Repeat,* was published in early 2007 and quickly established Bell as a leading voice in the mental health community. He is a sought-after motivational speaker and serves as a national spokesperson for the nonprofit International OCD Foundation (formerly the Obsessive Compulsive Foundation), to which he is donating a portion of this book's proceeds.

Visit Jeff Bell online at
www.BeyondTheDoubt.org